Sustaining a Resilient Asia Pacific Community

Sustaining a Resilient Asia Pacific Community

Edited by

Wilmar Salim and Kiran Sagoo

Cambridge Scholars Publishing

Sustaining a Resilient Asia Pacific Community, edited by Wilmar Salim and Kiran Sagoo

This book first published 2008 by

Cambridge Scholars Publishing

15 Angerton Gardens, Newcastle, NE5 2JA, UK

British Library Cataloguing in Publication Data
A catalogue record for this book is available from the British Library

ISBN (10): 1-84718-447-2, ISBN (13): 9781847184474

TABLE OF CONTENTS

LIST OF IMAGES

LIST OF TABLES

PREFACE

The annual International Graduate Student Conference of the East-West Center has evolved over the past decade from a small, in-house seminar to the largest gathering of its kind focused on the Asia Pacific region. In the past three years, the number of students presenting their scholarly work has topped 120 annually, drawn from more than 20 countries and 50 institutions of higher learning. The conference is entirely managed by graduate student fellows from the East-West Center. The East-West Center encourages this student initiative by providing conference space, a pool of willing professionals to help evaluate and select abstract submissions and serve as conference moderators and occasional guidance from Education and Fiscal Office staff. The Center makes available a modest total of $10,000 in travel support to participants from outside Hawai'i, which often enables students to secure matching support from their institutions. Beyond this, the conference is largely self-supporting, due in large part to the sweat-equity of our dedicated student community.

This volume, representing a cross-section of papers submitted to the 2006 Conference around the theme of resiliency in the Asia Pacific region, was undertaken at the invitation of the publisher, and represents a further evolution of public access to the scholarly thinking of bright graduate students drawn from around the world. The volume is anchored by a synthesizing essay by two past conference chairs, Wilmar Salim from Indonesia and Kiran Sagoo from Malaysia, both of whom are completing their Ph.D. degrees at the University of Hawai'i in Urban and Regional Planning and Sociology respectively, as East-West Center Graduate Degree Fellows. It is enhanced by the inclusion of Asian Studies Professor Barbara Andaya's thought-provoking keynote address to the Conference, the only one of the nine chapters not written by a graduate student.

The International Graduate Student Conference represents the essence of the East-West Center mission to stimulate the vigorous interchange of people and ideas between the Asia Pacific region and the United States. The reach of the Conference beyond those regions to other parts of the world demonstrates the unbounded and growing nature of interest in the Asia Pacific, and the resonance of a supportive forum from graduate student networking and collaboration.

Terance W. Bigalke (Ph.D.)
Director of Education
East-West Center, Honolulu

ACKNOWLEDGMENTS

The publication of this book could not be realized without the support of several people who contributed toward the conference organization and the preparation of this publication. We greatly thank Dr. Terance Bigalke, Ms. Mary Hammond, Ms. Mendl Djunaidy, Ms. Cindy Iwasaki and Ms. Stella Kolinski for their endless support during the preparation and implementation of the 5th East-West Center International Graduate Student Conference in February 2006. Dr. Charles Morrison's generous support in providing travel grants was highly appreciated, as it enabled us to bring in a large number of participants.

We would like to thank Mr. Richard Baker, Dr. Terance Bigalke, Dr. Gerard Finin, Dr. Sitiveni Halapua, Ms. Eileen Shea, and Dr. Peter Xenos for the time spent reviewing papers for this publication and providing suggestions to contributors to refine their chapters. Ms. Elisa Johnston's guidance through the publication and editorial process is highly appreciated. We would also like to thank Dr. Barbara Andaya who was the keynote speaker and kindly wrote up her speech for inclusion in this book. It is the guidance of senior scholars in the field and their collaboration with us that has enabled us to draw attention to the theme of community resilience, which has now materialized into a published form.

Lastly, we would like to thank editors and staff of Cambridge Scholars Publishing for encouraging us to turn the selected conference papers into a book. We hope that this publication, with the inclusion of the above theme and written from different perspectives, will ultimately expand the collection of social sciences literature that we wish to promote.

Wilmar Salim and Kiran Sagoo
November 2007

We would like to thank the following for permission to use previously published material.

University of California Press for permission to reproduce a map on page 187 of Martin W. Lewis and Kären E. Wigan. 1997. "The Myth of Continents: A Critique of Metageography," which appears here as Figure 2-1.

Journal of World History for a copy of map 3 on page 293 of Yang Bin, "Horses, Silver and Cowries: Yunnan in Historical Perspective," Vol. 15, No. 3, 2004, which appears here as Figure 2-2.

RoutledgeCurzon for permission to reproduce a map that Dai Yifeng used on page 22 of David Y. H. Wu and Sidney C. H. Cheung (eds.), 2002, "The Globalization of Chinese Food," (University of Hawai'i Press), which appears here as Figure 2-3.

PART I

PROJECTING A RESILIENT ASIA PACIFIC COMMUNITY

CHAPTER ONE

A RESILIENT ASIA PACIFIC COMMUNITY: ISSUES AND SOLUTIONS

WILMAR SALIM AND KIRAN SAGOO

Introduction

The Asia Pacific community has seen tremendous challenges in the past decades: political conflicts, economic crises, environmental deterioration, cultural and ethnic clashes, disease outbreaks, and natural and man-made disasters. Nevertheless, community resilience through these struggles is well noted, with many positive and successful case studies, both contemporary and historical, to learn from. Community resilience has been perceived commonly, as the hardiness of a community towards hazard or disaster. It is rare for this concept to be applied in other contexts. This book seeks to expand the concept of community resilience from not just overcoming environmental disaster to include other aspects such as political perseverance, community empowerment for better health and creating policies that incorporate local cultural values to facilitate development.

Adger (2000) provides a framework linking social and ecological resilience. He argues that the concept of resilience can be expanded to include vulnerability. Vulnerability, which encompasses disruption to livelihoods and a loss of security, can be observed at different scales and in a wide range of phenomena. Adger (2000) states that "resilience increases the capacity to cope with stress and is hence a loose antonym for vulnerability," therefore resiliency can be observed in the same way as vulnerability. He further defines social resilience as "the ability of communities to withstand external shocks to their social infrastructure" where the resilience of institutions and social capital are taken into consideration. This basic framework establishes a foundation for us to proceed by projecting the concept of a resilient community at different scales and in different circumstances, loosely bounded by a geographical area called Asia Pacific.

Coming out of an established international graduate student conference organized by the East-West Center, this book presents selected papers written by graduate students from different fields of study. After identifying historical or contemporary issues in each field, these papers propose a framework for resolving these issues, whether through global commitment, regional cooperation, national policy, or local knowledge and practice. The unifying thread of this book is sustaining resilience in the Asia Pacific.

Thus what is important here is that we acknowledge this perseverance and try to sustain and then disseminate it so that other communities may learn from these practices and experiences. The purpose of the conference was to address these issues and provide an avenue for dialogue. Generally, a volume like this would address the challenge of this region from a security, economics or political perspective. This book hopes to add to the literature on social resilience by addressing these issues from multidisciplinary and multilevel perspectives.

A general conclusion that can be drawn from this dialogue is that the level of connectedness, either between one community and another, or between a community and its ecosystem, determines the level of resilience of a community. This can be traced from brief discussions of each individual paper in the following section, which also provides the structure for the book.

Volume Content

Papers selected for this book focus on how the Asia Pacific community deals with issues at the local, national, and regional level. Cross-sectionally, these papers converge on multidisciplinary research areas: politics/international relations, judiciary, environment, health, economics, indigenous people, women empowerment, and education. The case studies discussed in this book also represent different countries and regions in Asia and the Pacific.

The chapters in the book are divided into four parts. Part One: Projecting a Resilient Asia Pacific Community frames the Asia Pacific and challenges the existing boundaries. Dr. Barbara Andaya's keynote address is presented in chapter two. She challenges the classical world divisions by arguing that historically global connection and interaction of "virtual communities" have been sustained for centuries. However, academic, diplomatic and strategic formulations of "world areas" have worked to separate Asia from the Pacific, rather than bringing these regions together. Given this heritage, it has not been easy to create, or even to think about, much less sustain, a truly interactive "Asia Pacific" community. There are however, important nodes of connection that make it possible to think conceptually about the ways in which people and societies living in different cultures and in different geographic regions have been brought together. In this context, we can profitably return to reconsiderations of the historical dimensions of globalized trade, and to the implications of this trade in regard to the movement of objects and the *imaginaire* of the individuals and communities involved. In tracking three examples of "trade products," her paper sets a context for further discussion in this volume by recognizing that the combination of human ingenuity, collaboration and common interests fundamentally challenges the academic confines of "area studies" boundaries.

Part Two: Regional Dynamics and Cooperation addresses the concept of community at the regional level. It focuses on cross-boundary issues from the perspective of politics and international relations, especially the power game played by nations external to the region. Both chapters in this section portray the interplay between external and internal powers, representing Southeast Asia and the Pacific regions.

The post–Cold War era witnessed contradictory positions in Southeast Asia. Existing regional tensions converged with the Soviet Union's dissolution, the US' rolling back, and the rising of China led to predictions that this region would be subject to conflicts. However, reality has proven otherwise. Southeast Asia has enjoyed independence and autonomy with moderate influence of external powers. This has led to debates about the origins of Southeast Asia's success, particularly the role of self-motivated foreign policies of Southeast Asian countries (ASEAN countries) and whether this situation will last in the near future. The chapter written by Ha Anh Tuan is intended to find appropriate answers to these questions. It argues that Southeast Asia's success in exercising a balance of power at the end of the Cold War prevented excessive domination by any one great power. By pursuing what he calls "balancing" policy in international relations, as a mode of resilience, the region enjoys its peace and autonomy and the outcome will be the same in the years to come.

Moving to the Pacific, Justin Liang writes about similar power dynamics ongoing in this ocean, influenced by external powers. For nearly three decades, Taiwan and China have been embroiled in extraterritorial rivalries within several Pacific island countries. Now, with hostility between the two raising to near boiling point in light of recent cross-strait developments, their struggle for dominance in the region is especially pronounced. Within many of these tiny island countries, a real-life match of *Go* is being played out between China and Taiwan—a game of diplomatic one-upmanship that exposes the friction looming latently, but impatiently, between the archrivals. This chapter examines the significance and implications of the Taiwan-China rivalry in the Pacific.

By critically investigating the more recent diplomatic clashes, Liang outlines what the current interests are for both countries and relates the implications of their conflicting interests. It argues that while a shift in the regional balance of power is certainly a conceivable consequence of the Taiwan-China rivalry in the South Pacific, it is but a distant one; a more pressing and immediate concern is the possibility of heightened regional instability actuated by the impulsive and often misinformed diplomatic decisions of island statesmen, who appear increasingly willing to buy into the corruptive checkbook politics of both Taiwan and China. Ultimately, the current stakes are highest not for the bigger players—China, Taiwan, the United States, Australia, and Japan—but for the vulnerable island nations themselves, who have both the most to gain and the most to lose from their diplomatic engagements with the "two Chinas."

From the delicate balancing of powers in Southeast Asia and the Pacific, Part Three: The Emerging Volatility, addresses growing concerns at the national level. Anthea Moore discusses how the contradictory concepts of land in Melanesian and Western cultures have contributed to the Bougainvillean crisis over the Panguna mine. The implementation of the Western understanding of land as a commodity versus the Melanesian perception of land as identity has resulted in violent conflict, which has been further fueled by the absence of a strong state. It is unfortunate that current economic principles which uphold property rights as a precondition for development have only served to weaken prevailing social structures. Moore argues that the economic solution of providing monetary compensation for land usage is inadequate as land is so closely tied to one's identity in Melanesian societies. Therefore, to avoid conflict and promote development, there is a need for indigenous concepts of land to be incorporated into development policy.

She suggests that solutions may be found that allow these concepts to be reconciled in a way that uphold the values of indigenous communities and also not diminish the quality of economic property rights. She emphasizes a need to work with, rather than challenge, non-transferable indigenous customary land usage rights. Nevertheless, while these approaches have potential to address the prevailing problems, there is still a need to overcome orthodox economic principles. She argues that since the concept of land as identity is outside the economic paradigm, perhaps solutions to this conflict may also be found outside the economic paradigm. It is also necessary for any changes to land tenure be implemented slowly and carefully.

Matt West's chapter is based on another type of conflict, the protection of intellectual property rights, while enabling people to have a livelihood and access to goods they would otherwise not be able to afford. His observational study of movie and music disc piracy in Xi'an, China highlights the difficulties involved in protecting intellectual property due to public perception of pirated movie and music discs being seen primarily as a retail business.

He explains that despite China having a 100-year history with intellectual property laws, the concept of ownership of intangible ideas remains to be constructed. He argues that imposing a Western style concept of intellectual property laws makes it almost unenforceable, resulting in confusion among consumers. His research in Xi'an illustrates that there is no proper way to distinguish between licensed and pirated discs for music and movies. Movie and music discs sold at large chain stores at higher prices were merely higher quality pirated products and not licensed discs. Consumers were sometimes confused as to whether these discs were licensed or pirated copies.

In order to formulate and implement effective policy, he states that it is necessary to understand how piracy operates in the local context. He argues that the United States, China and other governments need to be willing to adapt intellectual property laws closer to local practices. Unlike Western perception of piracy being an organized crime, consumers, retailers and the police in Xi'an view businesses selling pirated discs as a business. In fact, certain respondents saw these businesses as enabling them to take part in a global culture by providing movies and music at a price they would otherwise not be able to afford.

West's proposed solution reflects a similar principle observed in Moore's chapter: Western frameworks need to be adapted to a local context in order for there to be a feasible solution. Similar to Moore's argument that a solution to a conflict may lie outside of established norms, West also suggests that other options and systems need to be explored in relation to the protection of intellectual property. Only by developing a country's store of intellectual property can proper protection measures be put in place.

Part Four of this book provides a multidisciplinary perspective on community perseverance with case studies from Sri Lanka, Vietnam and Fiji. Mamiit-Coburn and Wijayaweera provide an assessment of different communities in Sri Lanka and illustrate the importance of mangroves ecosystem for community survival during natural disasters such as the Indian Ocean tsunami in December 2004. Sri Lanka encompasses a diversity of coastal mangroves which provide a wide array of goods and services, ranging from fishery, forest products and tourism to shoreline protection. The tsunami substantially and, unfortunately, tragically demonstrated the shoreline protection function of mangrove ecosystems. Early reports after the tsunami showed that mangroves provided protection and reduced the impact of destruction on coastal communities. The damage brought by the tsunami to coastal villages exhibited the need to assess the role of mangroves as life and property saving belts. This study presents a post-tsunami community assessment of the shoreline protection function of mangroves in Southern Sri Lanka.

The availability of household damage cost information allowed the use of a comparative damage cost assessment approach to estimate the shoreline protection value of mangrove ecosystems. Through household surveys, this study assessed the socioeconomic impacts of the tsunami disaster on coastal livelihoods at the villages of Kapuhenwala and Wanduruppa. The village of Kapuhenwala exhibits healthy and intact mangrove ecosystems, whereas, disturbed and degraded mangrove ecosystems characterizes the village of Wanduruppa. The community assessment estimated a higher incidence of damage costs in areas with degraded mangrove vegetation.

By minimizing the variation in the two study sites and adjusting the differences into common units, the results indicate that cost of damages to livelihood and property in Wanduruppa are approximately ten times the costs of damages in Kapuhenwala. The damage costs avoided appraisal suggests that threatened mangroves reduce the protection afforded to inland properties, community infrastructures and livelihood. The findings also indicate the economic rationale of including mangrove rehabilitation efforts in the post-tsunami reconstruction and rebuilding programs. It would suggest that natural ecosystems can provide support system for community resilience, physically as well as economically.

Huong Tran's field study on a rural village in Vietnam illustrates the importance of community participation in improving primary health care. Prior to the implementation of a community based primary health care project, about 63 percent of women did not receive prenatal care and home births was at 45 percent. Significant improvements were seen after the project had been implemented for two years. Eighty percent of women received prenatal care, with 81 percent of deliveries taking place in the health center. An essential component to the success of the project was strong community participation.

In this chapter, Huong Tran discusses the factors that were essential in building community participation. The volunteers were involved in the project from its inception which provided a sense of ownership and responsibility. Being supported and valued by their families and community was another source of encouragement. Participants were further empowered through training sessions. This participatory process was particularly empowering to ethnic minority volunteers as it inferred a strong sense of acceptance by the community.

Huong Tran's study illustrates a successful outcome in setting up a sustainable health network to build community resilience for better health. Once again, the recognition and incorporation of local values into an established Western framework was crucial to the success of this project. By recognizing and utilizing the social capital present in the form of love for the homeland and Buddhist principles of contribution, a sustainable health network based on the principles of volunteerism could be created.

Kevin Chang's chapter focuses on the difficult struggle Fiji has faced in seeking justice and reconciliation, and maintaining political stability. Resiliency at the national level remains shaky, as seen by the country's experience of four coups over the past twenty years. The need for a process of justice to heal wounds inflicted by past coups, especially with the 2000 coup which resulted in a high degree of violence, remains unheard. Chang states that the failure of the reconciliation process has been due to not being able to bring to justice the perpetrators of violence and not providing fair reparation to its victims. The reconciliation process promoted by Laisenia Qarase's SDL Coalition Government was seen as being cosmetic and marginalizing to a section of Fiji's society.

He argues that the absence of a process to promote peace and democratization only served to weaken Fiji's reconciliation process. He suggests that for there to be a sustainable solution, it is necessary for all ethnic communities in Fiji be ensured fair and equitable social and economic participation, and have an opportunity to learn from its recent history of violence.

Chang's case study clearly illustrates the principle of the strength of community resilience being dependent on the level of connectedness between one community with another. Ethnic tensions between Fiji's major ethnic groups have only served to weaken community resilience at the national level. In contrast, Huong Tran's study which showed a high level of connectedness between villagers resulted in a positive outcome for everyone concerned.

The discussions in this book expand the concept of community resilience to show its dependence on the interconnectedness between nations, communities and the environment. While community resilience remains tested in certain countries and regions, it is uplifting to see it thriving in other areas. Ranging from regional stability in adopting successful balance of power strategies, to the well-being of communities in successfully mobilizing their social capital or adopting sound environmental strategies, community resilience continues to grow and develop in the Asia Pacific region.

Works Cited

Adger, W. Neil. 2000. "Social and ecological resilience: are they related?" *Progress in Human Geography*, Vol. 24, No. 3, 2000, pp 347-364.

CHAPTER TWO

CHALLENGING WORLD AREA DIVISIONS: THE ASIA PACIFIC COMMUNITY

BARBARA WATSON ANDAYA

The historical processes by which the global community remains divided into world areas provides the provocative theme for the 1997 publication, the *The Myth of Continents*, by Martin Lewis and Kären E. Wigan. A significant feature of the Lewis-Wigan argument is the assertion that the conceptual boundaries between "Pacific," "Melanesia," "Southeast Asia," "East Asia," "South Asia" have become entrenched in diplomatic, international and academic thinking. Indeed, like many of my colleagues, I have often been frustrated by the extent to which these divisions have militated against cross-cultural cooperation and research. One could even argue that in the realities of academe an interactive "Asia Pacific community" is actually quite difficult to locate, much less to sustain. Against this background, it is encouraging to see the ways in which the essays included here signal the collegiality and co-operation that can open up avenues to more inclusive conversations.

In early 2006, when I was asked to talk to the East-West Center graduate student conference on which this volume is based, I was initially at a loss to think of something to say that would be in keeping with the overall theme, and at the same time true to my own credentials. Yet on reflection, I felt I might have something to offer. Although I am a historian of Southeast Asia in the seventeenth and eighteenth centuries, I have a broader interest in the problems and potentialities of "crossing borders" between disciplines and between geographic areas. The global divisions that Lewis and Wigan describe project an academic rigidity and insensitivity to historical realities. However, I strongly believe that the divisions they identify have in fact been countered by the myriad ways in which human ingenuity has responded to the demands of international markets. The movement of people, goods and ideas over vast distances has fostered global connections that are often centuries old, sustaining the interaction of what we might today consider "virtual communities."

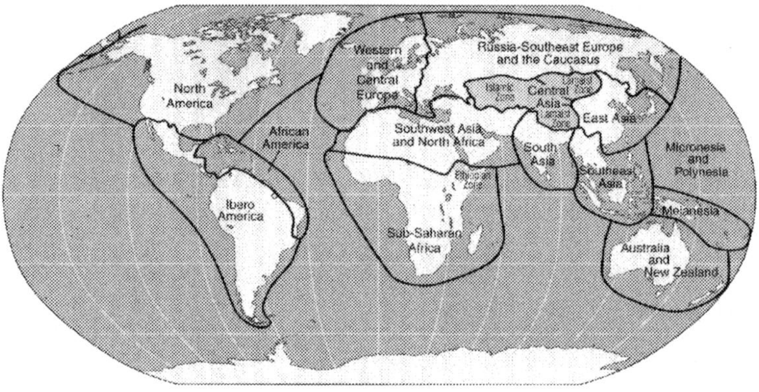

Figure 2-1 Lewis and Wigan's world areas (from Lewis and Wigan 1997)

In pursuing this line of argument, I turned to some of my own interests. In studying the history of global trade I never cease to be amazed by the extent to which human beings can co-operate in bringing desired products from their place of origin to a quite different place of consumption. In my presentation to the conference delegates I took three separate "trade products" and tracked their movement across different areas. My purpose was to demonstrate that there are historical linkages across "Asia" and with the "Pacific," and that the human creativity and imagination which supported these links should encourage us to think about connections between societies in the past, and how these can be reformulated and maintained in modern times.

Cowries

My first product was the cowry shell. Today we hardly think of cowries as a form of money, but in early times they were highly prized both as a sign of status and a medium of exchange, not merely in Africa but through much of the non-Western world. In the Pacific, for example, the much-prized golden cowries were worn only by high chiefs and royalty; an early Thai law code specifies the amounts of cowries which can be levied as fines; in Bengal and northeast India cowries provided small change until the introduction of copper coins in the eighteenth century.

Although the species of cowry commonly used for money (*Cypraea moneta*) is widely distributed through the Indo-Pacific area, it was the Maldive islands, off the southwest Indian coast, that supplied *Cypraea moneta* for most of the world's trade in pre-modern times.

Of minor significance today, the Maldives came to trading prominence not only because its islands could supply an abundance of cowries, but also because the people there developed a simple and highly efficient means of collection. Bundles of coconut palm fronds were laid out in shallow lagoons, and the cowries grew on these, feeding on the layers of detritus that accumulated on the leaves. After some time the bundles were pulled out to the beach where the cowries died in the hot sun and could be shaken off on to the sand. They were then buried in a pit so that the flesh rotted away, allowing the collectors to gather the clean empty shells.

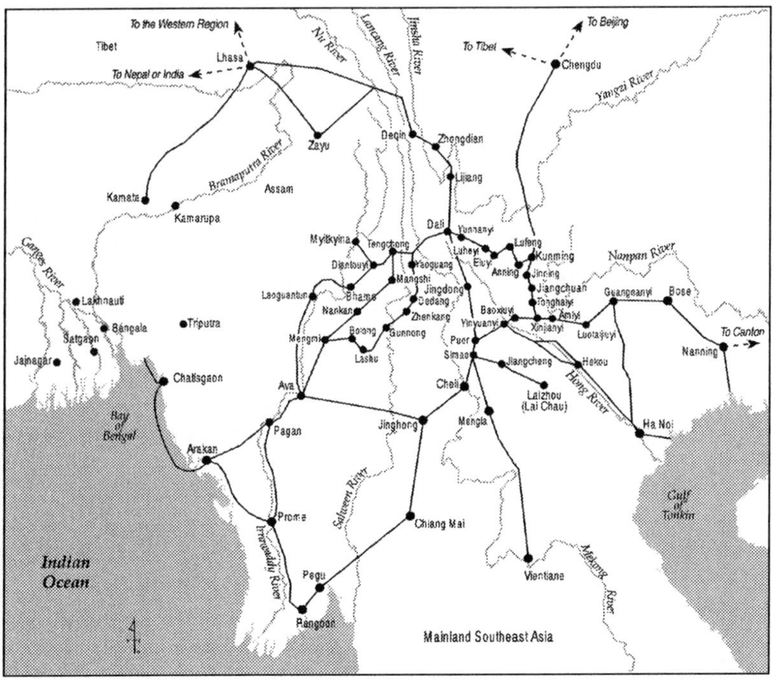

Figure 2-2 The cowry network 13th-19th centuries (from Bin 2004)

Nearly all the early travelers who visited the Maldives mentioned the importance of cowry exports, which were transported in bulk to Africa, India and much of mainland Southeast Asia. An interesting destination is Yunnan, which remained largely outside the Chinese monetary system, where cowries had long given way to metal coinage. From at least the ninth century cowries had been regarded as a prestigious form of exchange in Yunnan, especially among the elite, supplying clear evidence of close trading links with the Indian Ocean zone. Accumulated because of their value, cowries were used not merely for small purchases, but for larger transactions, like buying land and houses, submitting taxes, making donations to Buddhist churches, and paying government salaries. In other words, cowries in Yunnan fulfilled the functions of modern coinage, and only in the seventeenth century were they replaced by silver and copper coins.

These are various reasons for this shift. Throughout the Ming dynasty (fourteenth to seventeenth centuries), the arrival of over two million Han migrants dramatically changed Yunnan's demography. By the end of the Ming, Han Chinese were the ethnic majority in Yunnan. Ming efforts to replace cowries with copper cash were not always successful, but they did lead to the devaluation of cowries. In addition to Chinese insistence that taxes should be remitted in coinage, the expansion of trade markets made cowries less acceptable in larger transactions. To this was added the disruption of long-term trade networks with Bengal and coastal Southeast Asia because of an increased European presence, as well as the European perception that "currency" should always be metal-based. Yet a historian would also stress that Yunnan's cowry exchange system did persist for a considerable period, primarily because of the commerce that made southwest China an integral part of the Indian Ocean trade structure. We should also remember that this trade was supported and sustained by generations of fishermen and their families who collected the cowries, by merchants and shippers who took them across the oceans, and by traders who carried them via overland routes; it was a truly cross-cultural and cross-border project, but one that was driven by human enterprise.

Teripang

My second example was far less attractive. The first Western observers to encounter Indonesian *teripang*—also called *bêche-de-mer*, sea cucumber, or less politely but more descriptively, sea slug—were unanimous in their view that they were repulsive; one of the kinder descriptions likened them to "sausages which have been rolled in mud and then thrown up the chimney." Nonetheless, a history of this "repulsive" creature and its place in Asian trade requires us to think beyond the area studies boundaries that so often confine us. Even more, perhaps, such a history is a reminder of the great lengths to which human beings will go in order to satisfy the demands of commerce.

Teripang, or edible *holothuria*, are found throughout the world's oceans and there are in fact about 1200 known species. However, by far the greatest diversity and abundance occurs among the islands of Southeast Asia and adjacent areas—a Dutchman collecting material in the mid-nineteenth century, for instance, listed at least 112 different types, although not all of these were edible. They are usually visible lying on the sea floor or in areas exposed at low tide, so they could be collected both by gathering, by dredging, or by deep–sea fishing.

We know about the trade in *teripang* primarily because of a growing demand in China and Japan, although they were also a common food in eastern Indonesia and parts of the Pacific. The market was undoubtedly greatest in China, where they were used in soups, braised with vegetables, or fried. On one level, sea slugs (*haishen*) were valued for their jelly-like texture, which was said to bring out the flavor of other foods. More specifically, however, they were believed to contain elements beneficial to overall health and (presumably because of the phallic-like shape) were regarded as a potent aphrodisiac. By the eighteenth century, the inclusion of a dish containing *haishen* had become part of the accepted menu for Chinese feasts, like other exotic foods such as birds' nest and shark's fins. The most desired sea-slugs came from the *Nanhai,* the seas of Southeast Asia, especially around the islands of eastern Indonesia. As a Chinese tutor who traveled widely in the archipelago in the 1780s explained, "*Teripang* is one kind of insect living at the bottom of the sea. . . . The deeper the sea, the more and finer the *teripang* is" (Salmon 2003). Although *teripang* can be collected in tidal flats, the waters of eastern Indonesia are indeed deep. For example, the deepest point of the Java Trench, which stretches for 2,600 kilometers along the southwestern and southern Indonesian archipelago, is 7,450 meters below the water surface, nearly twice the average depth of the Indian Ocean.

While it is certainly true that Chinese junks and Chinese middlemen played a major role in carrying *teripang* to China, they were not the collectors. Collecting could be done both in the deep sea, where it was the work of men, but also along the shoreline, where women and children could be involved. From the late eighteenth century boats from Sulawesi, manned by Makassar and Bugis sailors, began to sail to the southern land that we now call Australia, and here the northern shores have become a major destination for *teripang* fishing. Stone fireplaces, tamarind trees, and Muslim graves supply material evidence of the Makassar/Bugis presence, but their influence can also be found in Aboriginal art, linguistic borrowings, and legend.

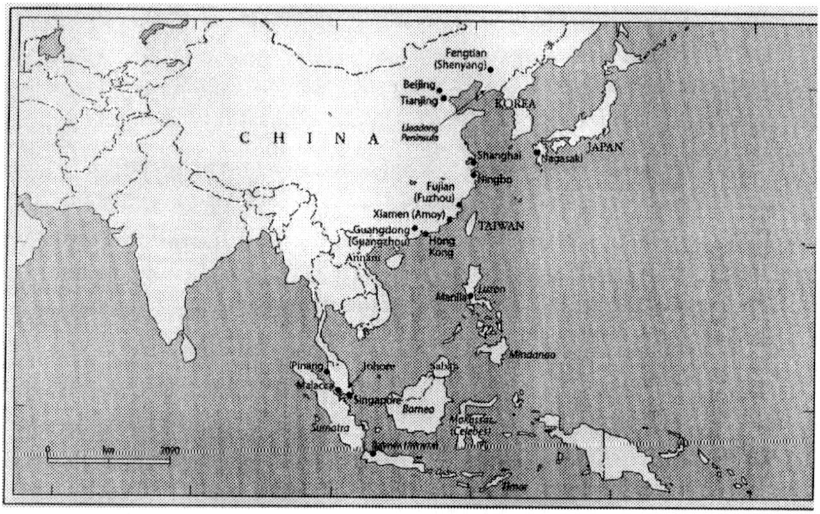

Figure 2-3 Sea slug sites in Southeast and East Asia (from Yifeng 2002)

As in the case of cowries, successful collection depended on traditional knowledge, for collectors had to be able to recognize the different varieties and their potential value, but must also have intimate knowledge of tidal movements and ocean currents. Recent anthropological work has shown that *teripang* fishermen still perform rituals considered crucial to a successful catch, and seek permission from the ancestors and goddess of the sea before they harvest. Without this supernatural support, the enterprise will surely fail.

Pineapples

The gathering of sea cucumbers, still important today, provides another instance of a complex relationship drawing societies in different parts of the world—people who have never seen each other—into a "community" that sustains a continuing connection. My third "trade product" was far more familiar to my audience: *Ananas comosus*, the botanical designation of the fruit we know as the pineapple. Although it is native to Brazil, Bolivia, and Paraguay, Christopher Columbus is credited with discovering the pineapple on the island of Guadeloupe in 1493. It was named for its resemblance to a pine cone, but the term "pineapple" did not appear in print until nearly two centuries later. The native word, *anana*, meaning "excellent fruit," provided the derivation for *ananas*, by which pineapple is known in many languages.

European voyaging between South America and Asia helped bring pineapples to India, Southeast Asia, and the West Indies. Spaniards introduced the pineapple into the Philippines and may have taken it to Guam early in the sixteenth century. It was apparently Captain James Cook who brought the pineapple to Hawai'i in 1790; the state's last plantations, which attracted so many migrant workers, are due to be phased out by 2008, a sobering comment on the effects of globalization.

What was the source of the pineapple's appeal? While there are many varieties—small, large, round, oval, green, orange, yellow, shiny or matt-surfaced—we all know that it can be a delicious dessert. When George Washington tasted pineapple in 1751 in Barbados, he declared it to be his favorite tropical fruit. However, it is worth remembering that the pineapple can also be used to supply a more pungent flavor. For instance, half-ripe pineapples are used in Vietnamese and Cambodian sour soups and Malaysian and Indonesian curries. Furthermore, the plant had other uses outside the kitchen. Pineapple leaves, long, wide, and relatively rigid, yield a strong fiber which was used extensively in various societies for making textiles and other items. It is remarkable how quickly people in tropical Asia learned to exploit this newly introduced fruit; for example, some communities encouraged the leaf growth of certain varieties by removing the young fruits. In Guangdong and on the island of Hainan pineapple fibers were woven into coarse textiles resembling grass cloth; in India the thread was prized by shoemakers; in Guam it was hand-twisted to make casting nets. However, probably the most famous area of production was the Philippines, where textiles made of *pina* cloth were and are highly esteemed.

Today pineapple crops are overwhelmingly planted for food, and tropical Asia dominates world production, led by Thailand and the Philippines. Global familiarity with a once-rare fruit, made possible by the ubiquity of canned pineapple transported across miles of ocean, is nicely captured in the 1951 ballet, "Pineapple Poll," where the central character (appealingly dressed in yellow and green), dances against a Portsmouth background of ships and sailors. In a very different context, and again very far from the tropics, the Norwegian scientist, mathematician, inventor and poet Piet Hein (1905-96) was even inspired to write one of his famous "grooks" or very short poems, "Love is like a pineapple; sweet and undefinable." Perhaps even more interesting is the fact that the pineapple symbol came to invoke ideas of warmth and friendliness, and was therefore used frequently in America to decorate bed posts, tablecloths, napkins, dinner tables—anything associated with welcoming guests. In Hawai'i today, despite the impending plantation closures, the pineapple remains a fitting motif for the hospitality industry, and pineapple-themed products still abound. From lamps to candle holders to salt and pepper shakers and beyond, representations of the pineapple, we are told, extend the greeting of "Welcome!"

My goal in talking about these three trade products was simple; I wanted to encourage my audience to think about the networks created by the combination of human desire and human ingenuity, networks that stretch across vast geographic regions and link people who had never seen each other. In his much-cited work, *Imagined Communities*, Benedict Anderson has talked about the processes that lead to a shared sense of nationhood among otherwise disconnected groups. I have been thinking about the interactions that could link a cowry fisherman in the Maldives to a trader in Hunan, or an Australian aboriginal who helped dry *teripang* to a wealthy Chinese Mandarin who served it in a banquet. Probably you will agree that my best example of a "global product" is the pineapple. And just as the pineapple is a symbol of hospitality throughout the world, it could also stand as a symbol for this conference, because both have transversed and connected the Asia Pacific region. In the United States the pineapple has become especially associated with Hawai'i, and it is fitting that the theme of the conference was the connectivity between Asia and the Pacific. The great challenge is to translate a concern with shared issues into personal associations, for it is the circulation and exchange of people which will in the end sustain a true Asia Pacific community. It is the fostering of lasting human relationships that lies at the heart of the East-West Center enterprise.

Works Cited

Anderson, Benedict R. O. 1983. *Imagined Communities: Reflections on the Origin and Spread of Nationalism.* London: Verso.

Bin, Yang. 2004. "Horses, Silver and Cowries: Yunnan in Historical Perspective," *Journal of World History*, Vol. 15, No. 3, pp 281-322.

Lewis, Martin W. and Kären E. Wigan. 1997. *The Myth of Continents: A Critique of Metageography*. Berkeley and London: University of California Press.

Salmon, Claudine. 2003. "Wang Dahai and His View of the "Insular Countries" (1791)," in Ding Choo Ming and Ooi Kee Beng (eds.), *Chinese Studies in the Malay World*. Singapore: Times Media, pp 31-67.

Yifeng, Dai. 2002. "Food Culture and Overseas Trade: The Teripang Trade between China and Southeast Asia during the Qing Dynasty," in David Y. H. Wu and Sidney C. H. Cheung (eds.), *The Globalization of Chinese Food*. Honolulu: University of Hawai'i Press, pp 21-42.

PART II

REGIONAL DYNAMICS AND COOPERATION

CHAPTER THREE

BALANCE OF POWER OF SOUTHEAST ASIAN COUNTRIES: ORIGIN OF PEACE AND AUTONOMY IN THE POST–COLD WAR ERA

HA ANH TUAN

Introduction

The post–Cold War era has witnessed a sea of change in world politics. In Southeast Asia, a power vacuum appeared after the Soviet Union's dissolution and United States' withdrawal from its last regional military bases of Subic Bay and Clark Air Force Base in 1991. China took this opportunity to expand its southward influence. A significant field is China's expansion in the South China Sea. In January 1992, Beijing adopted the "Law of the People's Republic of China on the Territorial Waters and Contiguous Areas," claiming that South China Sea is an undisputable part of its territory. This policy was followed by China's unilateral military and economic activities in disputed areas in the following years. This position has irritated Southeast Asian claimants including Vietnam, Malaysia, the Philippines, and Brunei. Within the region, suspicions between six old ASEAN countries and the other four Southeast Asian states still exist. Against this context, a scenario of Balkanization in Southeast Asia, referring to a situation in which the region becomes divided in conflicts and is strongly influenced by external powers, in the post–Cold War era was raised (Asia Society 2004).

However the reality since then has not been as what people imagined. Division between ASEAN-6 and Indochina was removed after the signing of the Peace Agreement for Cambodia Conflict in 1991. Vietnam's accession to ASEAN in 1995, followed by the entry of Laos and Myanmar in 1997 and Cambodia in 1999 marked a substantial change in international relations in Southeast Asia. In relationship to world powers, Southeast Asian countries have managed to maintain good relations with all powers. Regional peace and autonomy have also been maintained.

This condition has led to two questions. First, why have Southeast Asian countries (ASEAN countries) succeeded in maintaining regional independence and peace? Second, will this success continue in the short-term future and what should regional governments do, if anything, to ensure it? Constructivists highlighted the role of regionalism and regional frameworks such as the ASEAN and ASEAN Regional Forum (ARF) in fostering regional stability. Conversely, realists disclaim them, describing regional frameworks as talking shops. While Amitav Acharya asserts that ASEAN is a sort of a "nascent security community" (Acharya 2000: 5), Tobias Nischalke states that it is a "community of convenience" (Nischalke 2000).

This chapter argues that regional mechanisms are useful in that they serve as frameworks for ASEAN countries to exercise their broad balance of power. This leads to the main argument: because ASEAN countries have exercised a balance of power strategy successfully since the end of the Cold War, they have avoided excessive domination by any one great power. If they continue this policy successfully, the outcome will be the same in the years to come.

Three main factors that influence international relations in Southeast Asia in the post–Cold War era are (1) international structural change that favors regional peace and autonomy, (2) the pragmatic policies of ASEAN countries, and (3) the development of regionalism and regional mechanisms. While the first has created a favorable environment for regional countries to exercise their policies, the last two factors are characterized by the balance of power. I will argue that because the first factor will not change in the years to come, if the two last factors persist, or the balance of power is maintained, Southeast Asia will continue to enjoy the existing peaceful and independent environment.

Balance of Power and its Application to Southeast Asia

Balance of power is a term with many definitions. The development of this concept relies on the basic assumptions of a realist camp of thought that the international system is anarchical and the utmost motives for states are maximizing their national interests and security in a given context.

According to Michael Leifer (1996), the meaning of balance of power can be simplified into two categories. First, it is employed to describe a relationship between two or more states defined in terms of their relative capabilities. Second, it is understood as a policy aimed at preventing the establishment of undue dominance by one or more states. As a policy, balance of power, or balancing, is conducted under two forms: internal and external balancing (Brawley 2004: 76-85).

Internal balancing is the notion of developing one's own strength through economic development, social cohesion, and building of military capacity so that it has the sufficient capability to face challenges externally and internally.

The texts in the field of international relations, however, often refer to balance of power as external balancing. External balance of power denotes a country's foreign policy to ensure that "no one power is in a position to determine the fate of others" (Dibb 1995: 6). The methods of securing this objective include non-offensive coalitions, forming tacit understandings, and the use of international institutions to neutralize a rising or potentially threatening power.

It is argued that small and medium-sized states have broader foreign policy options than only balancing or bandwagoning when they are faced with a potential regional hegemony (Schweiller 1999). Some alternatives in Southeast Asia include hedging, engagement, and binding (Chong 2004; Roy 2005). However, these strategies are not out of the range of the balancing policy which, as previously defined, does not rule out the possibility of states cooperating with the threatening state itself.

In Southeast Asia, balancing policies of ASEAN countries have been implemented both at the national and regional levels. Regionally, ASEAN countries have exercised collective balance of power by engaging major powers in regional mechanisms such as ASEAN+3 and the ARF with ASEAN plays the leading role in these dialogues. Nationally, countries adopt mixed strategies that include balance of threat, engagement and hedging. Types of balancing vary not only from country to country but also from the specific threats and the timing.

International Structural Change

The first factor that has safeguarded the peace and autonomy of Southeast Asian countries in relation with external powers is structural change in Southeast Asia in favor of peace and regional autonomy in the post–Cold War era. After the withdrawal of Vietnamese troops in Cambodia, the Peace Agreement for Cambodia conflict, signed in Paris in 1991, led to the "normalization" between Indochina and ASEAN-6 countries. Since then, intra-ASEAN relations have been continually fostered. By 1999, the vision of an ASEAN of all ten Southeast Asian countries had been realized. Although ASEAN countries found themselves sandwiched between two great powers namely the United States and

China; these two giants, and other regional powers, have projected positive policies toward Southeast Asia.

During the Cold War period, China was a great concern for most Southeast Asian countries. Beijing's support to communist parties in Indonesia, the Philippines, and Thailand in their fight against their respective governments during 1960s made China a threat to these states. Sino-Vietnamese relation was viewed with suspicion. After the normalization in 1991, border demarcation and the conflicts in the South China Sea are always potential threats to the constructive and truthful Sino-Vietnamese relations.

China's behavior towards Southeast Asian countries, however, has changed since the end of the Cold War. Beijing's modern "grand strategy" requires it to uphold the *status quo* rather than challenge it. The strategy is composed of three components namely domestic stability and economic development, peaceful development, and good relations with the United States. This strategy requires the maintenance of status quo rather than changing it. In 1990, China decided to abandon the Khmer Rouge faction in Cambodia, paving the way for improved relations with ASEAN states. Subsequently, China's diplomatic relations with all ASEAN countries were quickly resumed. In the meeting of the ARF in 1995 in Brunei, China expressed its willingness to discuss and solve the South China Sea dispute according to international law. This was a breakthrough given that the South China Sea is one of the major obstacles for Sino-ASEAN relations. Previously, China refused to bring this issue into multilateral dialogues.

China's decision not to devaluate its currency in the regional financial crisis in 1997 and its active assistance to some ASEAN countries during that period has further proved China's ability and commitment to regional stability and development. In 2003, China signed the ASEAN Treaty of Amity and Cooperation (TAC), making it one of the first external countries to join in this treaty. Beijing also proposed the ASEAN-China Free Trade Area (ACFTA) in response to ASEAN's concerns over trade and investment diversion due to China's rising economic strength.

In relations with the United States, many ASEAN countries have been concerned about the credibility of U.S. commitment in Southeast Asia. After the collapse of the Soviet Union, Southeast Asia was no longer considered a priority in U.S. foreign policy. The United States closed its military bases in Subic and Clark in the Philippines in 1991 and was reluctant to assist Southeast Asia when the region fell into a financial crisis in 1997. However the United States has reasons to stay active in the region, especially after the September 11, 2001 terrorist attacks. Firstly, Southeast Asia has one of the largest and most important sea lanes in the world of which the safety and freedom to trade are of particular importance. Secondly, a Southeast Asia region of more than 500 million people is an important economic partner for the United States. Thirdly, the region is a strategic base which the United States can use to check China's geopolitical ambitions. Lastly, Southeast Asia is important in the U.S.-led global war on terrorism and retaining close relations with Southeast Asian countries is critical. In a meeting between ASEAN and the United States in Singapore in 1993, U.S. Secretary of State Warren Christopher reaffirmed America's active engagement in Asia which has recently been demonstrated by its close military ties with the Philippines, Singapore, and Thailand. In recent years, the United States has had regular joint military exercises with some regional countries.

Apart from China and the United States, other regional powers are also actively engaged in Southeast Asia. Japan is searching for a status in the region and the world. Support from Southeast Asian countries thus is the key for this projection. Its policy is to broaden its influence in Southeast Asia by strengthening Japan's cooperation in the fields of economics, culture, education, and human resource training. Another active actor in Southeast Asia is India. India has pursued a "Look East" policy, putting stress on the importance of close relations with the Southeast Asian region. As Indian Prime Minister Manmohan Singh noted: "I reiterate India's commitment to work with ASEAN and other East Asian countries to make the 21st century truly an Asian century" (Kuppuswamy 2006). This country, along with Australia and New Zealand, were the three external states attending the first East Asian Summit in Kuala Lumpur in December 2005. All regional powers—Australia, China, India, Japan, Pakistan, South Korea, and Russia—have joined in the ASEAN's Treaty of Amity and Cooperation.

In short, the influence of external powers in Southeast Asia is divided into two tiers. China and the United States, the most influential outsiders in the region lie in the upper one. The lower tier includes regional powers namely Japan, Australia, India, South Korea and Russia. The salient feature of this structure is that all powers positively act in a complex network of interconnected relations that prevent any one of them from having the willingness or capacity to break the *status quo*. This creates a favorable environment for ASEAN states to exercise their independent foreign policies.

Pragmatic Foreign Policy: Southeast Asian Countries

In this favorable regional context, pragmatism is the most outstanding feature in the foreign policy of ASEAN countries. This means that ASEAN countries conduct their foreign policies based on their respective calculations of national interests, of which the most important are peace, independence and economic development. To achieve this objective, ASEAN countries share the same view that a balanced relationship with both the United States and China is crucial. They "all acknowledge the critical strategic role of the U.S. in the region both in terms of security guarantees as well as economic ties ... [and] ha[ve] no choice but to engage with China, ... a 'true' regional great power" (Goh 2005: 3). Relations with other powers such as Japan, Australia and India are also developed to reduce the uncertainty caused by the strong influence of the two major powers. This maintains a balance of power in Southeast Asia.

Although sharing the idea of balance of power, ASEAN states employ different mixed strategies, depending on the particular issues and timing. In relations with China and the United States, the Philippines and Singapore "place greater emphasis and faith in their strategic relations with the U.S.," Indonesia and Malaysia "steer a middle course in between the U.S. and China," and "Thailand and Vietnam are most constrained by China strategically" (Goh 2005: 5). By policy categorization, Thailand has followed a hedging policy, while balancing against threat has been pursued clearly by the Philippines; and in more sophisticated manners, by Indonesia, Malaysia, and Vietnam. Singapore seeks a balance of power through engagement.

Hedging is employed by Thailand as a way to maintain good relations with China and the United States. As Chinawanno (2002) puts it, Thailand "moves adroitly between great power[s]...[to] maximize its relative gains and avert dependency." Because Thailand does not have any direct conflict of interests with China, the country is considered by China "as a 'bridge' to good relations and influence with the rest of Southeast Asia" (Bert 2003: 194). In February 1999, Thailand and China signed a Plan of Action for the 21st Century, a strategic partnership agreement which has included a regular exchange of military personnel and exercises and is considered as an informal bilateral military cooperation arrangement. Beijing increasingly becomes an important arms provider for Bangkok. Economic issues are also given a high priority in Sino-Thailand relations. After the downturn in 1997, Thailand has placed emphasis on improving economic ties with China. Both sides have signed a free trade agreement which took effect on October 2003.

In parallel, Thailand also has a formal collective defense with the United States. The U.S.-Thai military relationship is close in many ways, especially after the September 11, 2001 terrorist attacks in the United States. Bangkok has contributed troops to two military operations of the United States in Afghanistan and Iraq. Thailand has sent 130 troops to Afghanistan and 450 other to Iraq. In both cases, Thailand's troops only come in the reconstruction phase. Bilateral military relations is in the form of exchanging intelligence and holding over 40 joint military exercises annually, which include *Cobra Gold*, America's largest combined military exercise in Asia (Chanlett-Avery 2005). In 2003, the United States granted Thailand the status of non-NATO major ally. The two countries are currently undertaking free trade area negotiations.

Singapore attaches great strategic importance in its relationship with the United States. Singapore's economic structure makes it a natural ally with the United States. Singapore Prime Minister Goh Chok Tong stated that the United States and Singapore share interests "in the short term, medium term and in a strategic sense" (Chin 2004: 117). In 1998, the two sides made an addendum to the U.S.-Singapore Memorandum of Understanding of 1990. In July 2005, the United States and Singapore signed a strategic agreement named U.S.-Singapore Strategic Framework Agreement for a Closer Cooperation Partnership in Defense and Security to strengthen bilateral defense cooperation. Singapore hosts the U.S. Navy's Western Pacific logistics command and has upgraded its Changi Naval Base for visiting U.S. aircraft carriers. It also supported the United States' proposal to be involved in policing the Straits of Malacca (which was later turned down by Malaysia and Indonesia) and has participated in multilateral joint military exercises with the United States such as *Cobra Gold* and *Cope Tiger*. Bilateral free trade agreement between the two sides was signed in May 2003.

Although having close ties with the United States, Singapore's autonomy is safeguarded by balancing all involved powers. As Lee Kuan Yew put it, "if there is no such thing as balance of power in the Pacific, we are very much at risk" (*Far Eastern Economic Review* 1999: 34). For that reason, defense networking with friendly powers remains an important aspect of Singapore's defense policy. Since the post–Cold War, Singapore has had good relations with China in both military and economy. Despite having a close relationship with Taiwan, Singapore always gives priority to its relationship with China and adheres to a one China policy. Singapore's relations with Beijing are, along with Thailand, the best among all the ASEAN states (Bert 2003: 179). Its significant defense relations with other powers such as Britain and Australia are also maintained. Singapore is a member of the Five Powers Defense Agreement, of which four other members are the United Kingdom, Australia, Malaysia, and New Zealand.

Unlike Thailand and Singapore, Indonesia, Malaysia, the Philippines, and Vietnam have concrete concerns about the threat of China in the South China Sea.[1] The Philippines relies on the United States as a balance against China's threats, especially after the "mischief" incident. In May 1995, Manila found that Chinese troops had taken control over the reef claimed by the Philippines. It raised the idea that without U.S. support, Philippines' security might be at risk. After this incident, Manila revitalized its military relationship with the United States and signed the Visiting Force Agreement (VFA) with the United States in 1999. The VFA has opened the way for the resumption of American military support to the Philippines and to joint military exercises between the two countries. This tie evolved into a formal alliance when the Philippines obtained the position of a U.S. major non-NATO ally in 2003.

The Philippines also understands, however, that engaging with China is important to maintain peace and avoid dependence on the United States. In 1995, China and the Philippines signed a code of conduct to regulate their actions in the South China Sea. Although Beijing continued its unilateral actions by building up new facilities in the disputed reefs and islands it possessed, Manila has made efforts to strengthen its diplomatic relations with China. In 2000, the two sides signed an agreement on bilateral cooperation entitled "The Sino-Philippines Framework for Bilateral Cooperation in the 21st Century." In reality, they have enhanced cooperation through increased defense exchanges and by jointly combating crime.

Indonesia, Malaysia and Vietnam are more subtle in their external balance of power. Although they see China as a significant potential threat to regional stability, they do not want to antagonize China. This explains the fact that although they support military presence of the United States in the region, their defense ties and cooperation with the United States are either limited or kept secret. The close but quiet military cooperation between Malaysia and the United States was revealed when Malaysian Defense Minister Najib Tun Razak wrote: "For many years U.S. and Malaysian forces have cooperated on a wide range of missions with virtually no fanfare or public acknowledgement" (Razak 2002). The two

---

[1] Indonesia is not a claimant in South China Sea, but China's claim over Natuna water created great concern and suspicion over China's long term goals in Indonesia.

countries have regular joint military trainings and exercises in the air, on land and at sea. Many other cooperative activities have been conducted.

Indonesia and Vietnam also have a tacit policy of supporting U.S. military presence in the region for fear that if a rising China is not checked by another power it would be a threat to regional stability. On the other hand, they have suspicions about a U.S. threat. Indonesia's perception of the U.S. threat is that the United States may use the slogan of democracy and human rights to intervene in its internal affairs (Roy 2005: 136). This is likely to happen given that separatist movements are continuing in many parts of this country. The Communist Party of Vietnam considers "peaceful evolution" caused by the United States and the West as one of its four greatest challenges. Under these circumstances, Jakarta and Hanoi see the balance of relations between China and the United States as the best way to avoid threats from both countries, and be able to maintain their independence and stability. Indonesia resumed security ties with the United States in 2004 despite the fact that the U.S. military sanction imposed against Indonesia is still effective. At the same time, Indonesia also reached an agreement with China on military training cooperation. In 2004, the two countries agreed to build a strategic partnership.

Vietnam has moved in a similar path. Hanoi's relationship with Washington has rapidly improved in the last decade. Both Clinton and W. Bush, two recent presidents of the United States have visited Vietnam. In return, Vietnamese Prime Minister Phan Van Khai and Vietnamese President Nguyen Minh Triet paid visits to the United States in 2005 and 2007. Since 2003, Vietnam and the United States have exchanged high level military officials and several U.S. vessels have visited Vietnam for the first time since 1975. Vietnam-U.S. economic relations have also developed to an unprecedented level. Vietnam-U.S. bilateral trade agreement went into force in December 2001. One month after Vietnam's accession to the WTO in November 2006, U.S. Congress passed the Permanent Normal Trade Relations (PNTR) status with Vietnam, fully normalizing their bilateral relationship.

At the same time, Hanoi seeks to assure Beijing that its relationship with the United States is not too close so as to threaten China's stake. History has proved that whenever its relationship with China is down, Vietnam does not enjoy peace and stability. As it pursues the process of renovation, Vietnam's diplomatic relations with China was normalized in 1991. The two sides have exchanged high level officials regularly since the late 1990s. In 2005, the two countries signed a security accord, which led to the first high-level security talks in April of the same year.

Regionalism and Regional Mechanisms: Collective Balance of Power

ASEAN and regionalism in Southeast Asia have been thought of as a model of success for small and medium countries in different parts of the world. The development of regionalism and regional frameworks such as ASEAN and ASEAN Regional Forum is in essence a consequence of balancing foreign policy of ASEAN countries. Its importance however, deserves a separate analysis. It could be argued that regional frameworks have served as the ground for ASEAN as a grouping to pursue balance of power collectively.

To begin with, the sense of regionalism and regional frameworks themselves are means of balancing because it gives regional countries a higher position in dealing with external powers. A unanimous voice of ASEAN in regional issues clearly has more weight than the separate positions of its members. The accession of three Indochina countries to ASEAN has brought this grouping to a new height. There is opinion that the inclusion of Myanmar to ASEAN is a failure of the grouping because it causes more trouble than benefit to this association in its relations with Western countries. The acceptance of Myanmar to the group nevertheless has strategic meaning in strengthening the sense of regional unity and limit China's influence in the region. The driving seat of ASEAN in ARF can be achieved only when ASEAN countries unite themselves as a grouping. It is similar in the case of ASEAN+3, and East Asian Summit from December 2005. In ASEAN's 13th Summit in the Philippines in January 2007, ASEAN leaders decided to form an ASEAN Community by 2015, five years ahead of schedule. This is a concrete manifestation of ASEAN's consolidation amid worries that ASEAN cooperation will be diluted by a broader East Asia integration in the years to come.

Moreover, ASEAN as a grouping has pursued the balance of power within regional frameworks. Its policy is to create a condition to include external powers in regional mechanisms of which they have a stake to act upon existing principles. This will stop any one power from having the intention to move towards unilateralism, thus threatening regional peace and stability. The idea of balancing in the first place targets China and the United States. The strategy works on the basis that both countries do not want to stay out of regional security discussions. China's statement in the ARF meeting in Brunei in 1995 of being willing to deal with disputes over the South China Sea according to international law is an encouraging movement for ASEAN. ASEAN and China then signed the Declaration on the Conduct (DOC) of Parties in the South China Sea in 2002, making further effort to settle one of the toughest obstacles in Sino-ASEAN relations peacefully.

The balancing strategy of ASEAN is clearly demonstrated in the ARF mechanism. By setting up a regional forum, ASEAN countries intend to draw all powers in the Asia Pacific into the dialogue. Presently, all major powers including the United States, China, Russia, Japan, Australia, European Union, and others are members of the forum. As it is stated, a key purpose of the ARF was:

> "to engage the United States, Japan, and the PRC [China] in a structure of multilateral dialogue in order to promote a stable distribution of power in the Asia-Pacific. This core ASEAN objective has not changed since the formation of the forum… For ASEAN, the issue… is how to maintain a stable balance of the major powers" (Emmers 2001: 280).

The involvement of India in the forum in 1996 was also influenced by a balancing calculation. India is considered a countervailing power to Chinese ambitions in Asia. ASEAN's decision to enlarge the geographical scope of the forum was not welcomed by the United States, but was viewed as beneficial when the long-term involvement of the United States in Southeast Asia is uncertain (Emmers 2001: 282).

ASEAN's pursuit of a balance of power is consistent even without the presence of the United States. This was the case of the first East Asian Summit held in Malaysia in December 2005. In the negotiation period, China had wanted to exclude other external countries from participating in the regional meeting. In other words, only ten ASEAN countries and three Northeast Asian states, namely China, Japan and the Republic of Korea (South Korea) were to be members, giving China an opportunity to dominate the process and decisions of the Summit. Without the presence of the United States, ASEAN insisted that Australia, New Zealand and India be included in the meeting. The success of the bid diminished China's enthusiasm for the meeting because it created a balance of power that prevented China from dominating the Summit's agenda.

International Relations of Southeast Asian Countries: A Prospect

As previously discussed, the future of Southeast Asian autonomy depends on the continuity of the three mentioned factors: (1) the international and regional structure that favors regional peace and autonomy, (2) the balancing policy of ASEAN countries, and (3) the development of regionalism and regional mechanisms as a means of collective balancing. Researching these three factors, the first is likely to be stable. Because there will be no major shift of relative strength among major powers in the coming years, if pragmatic policies and regionalism in Southeast Asia are to be upheld, or the balance of power carried out successfully, the region will continue to enjoy peace and independence in the years to come.

Wayne Bert (2003) predicts that China would be the most likely power to replace the United States in "guarding" Southeast Asia's security. But this scenario is unlikely to happen in the short-term future. Strategically, China's "grand strategy" still requires it to uphold peace and *status quo* rather than challenge the role of the United States in the coming years. Economically, China can only overcome the United States in the next few decades if it continues to grow at a high speed while the U.S. economy reaches a deadlock. But the U.S. economy has continually grown since the early 1990s (except for a slow-down in the first years of George W. Bush's administration). Although China has had high economic growth in the past few decades, its economic and military capacity is far behind the United States. In 2004, China's GDP was nearly US$1,650,000 billion while the U.S. GDP was over US$11,650,000 billion. These figures in 2005 are around US$2,229,000 billion and US$12,455,000 billion respectively (World Bank 2005). If this trend continues, China still cannot overtake the United States in the next two decades. Although China is a large economy in absolute terms, it is still a developing country with more than 150 million people falling below the international poverty line. The nation also faces serious problems for economic and military development such as potential lack of energy and natural resources, serious environmental erosion, and the inability to access crucial advanced technology, which is crucial for economic and military capacities. Taking all of them into account, China is unable to compete with the United States in the near future.

Moreover, the idea of a loss of America's influence in Southeast Asia partly stems from the regional monetary crisis in 1997-98 when the increasing role of China in Southeast Asia was acknowledged. While the United States was reluctant to help ASEAN countries, China gave its neighbors a large sum of money for assistance (Mathews 2003). This was only one among the few cases when the United States showed its unwillingness to get involved in regional issues. In fact, the U.S. military presence in the region has further expanded. Apart from aforementioned ties with the Philippines, Thailand and Singapore, the United States' presence in East Asia and the Asia Pacific has also been reinforced. This is demonstrated in the U.S. commitment to protect Taiwan in 1996, the revision of U.S.-Japanese alliance in 2004, the deployment of nuclear-powered submarines and the stockpiling of conventional cruise missiles at Guam between 2002 and 2004. One may argue that the growing influence of the United States in Southeast Asia since 2001 is a loss to China. This development however helps to reinforce the *status quo* rather than challenge it. The recent increasing U.S. presence in Southeast Asia is only reinforcing its existing sphere of influence but not at the expense of China's sphere of influence.

Other regional powers are increasingly active in their engagements in Southeast Asia. Japan will continue its engagement in the region because the stability of Southeast Asia plays a crucial role in Japan's prosperity. However, Japan cannot challenge China's role in Southeast Asia. Japan's position will still be attached to that of the United States in regional issues. India and Australia have also shown their commitments to Southeast Asia through their active roles in the ARF and other regional mechanisms. The participation of Asia Pacific powers in the region through both bilateral and multilateral channels has created a condition that in the coming years no one power will have the willingness or capability to challenge the current power structure in Southeast Asia. This means that regional independence is contingent upon their continual success in their existing policy of balance of power.

The future of regional autonomy and stability however faces several challenges. Although Sino-U.S. relations in essence will remain stable, new developments in the region may create sharp changes in regional structure. In the first place, any miscalculation in Taiwan's course of independence will bring about conflicts between China and the United States. North Korea's nuclear weapon program is possibly another source of regional instability as it may trigger a regional arms race and the possibility of Japan's re-militarization cannot be ruled out.

Moreover, ASEAN countries must be careful in balancing domestic and external factors. They need to maximize national interests by strengthening their relationship with external powers and be aware of domestic sentiments. The positions of the Philippines and Indonesia in the U.S.-led global war on terror are clear examples. Manila's withdrawal of troops from Iraq to save the life of one Filipino civilian at the expense of its relations with the United States in 2005 and Jakarta's reluctance in supporting the U.S. global war on terror because of anti-American sentiment in its Muslim population demonstrate that domestic and external factors may run contrast to each other and they must be balanced.

The final challenge is the balance between strategic interests of regionalism and immediate interests of bilateral arrangements. As it has been analyzed, the sense of regionalism has a strategic importance in maintaining a high position for ASEAN countries in both bilateral and multilateral frameworks, but bilateral relations with external powers often bring about immediate benefits to regional countries. This requires Southeast Asian governments to keep strategic thought in mind in their policy-making calculations.

Conclusion

In short, structural change in the post–Cold War period has created favorable conditions for ASEAN countries to successfully maintain a balance of power. All major powers including China and the United States have a stake in maintaining good relations with regional governments. Although the regional context is favorable for balancing policy, it is not the determining factor. The policy of balance of power implemented by Southeast Asian countries has helped in maintaining autonomy and stability in the region.

Balancing policy is performed both at national and regional levels. Nationally, ASEAN governments have implemented both internal and external balancing. The latter is characterized by the balance of Southeast Asia's relations with China and the United States. Other external powers are also welcomed to promote a certain level of interdependence in the region. The sense of regionalism serves as a ground for ASEAN to balance power between the major nations. This policy has safeguarded regional peace and autonomy since the end of the Cold War.

Because the regional power structure is not likely to change in the short-term, if ASEAN countries successfully maintain their balance of power, the region will continue to enjoy a peaceful and independent environment. To ensure continual success, ASEAN governments need to balance relationships between economic development and military capacity building, between internal and external priorities and between regionalism and bilateral ties with external powers.

Works Cited

Acharya, Amitav. 2005. *The Quest for Identity: International Relations of Southeast Asia*, Oxford: Oxford University Press.

Asia Society and the U.S. National Intelligence Council. 2004. *Conference Report on Northeast and Southeast Asia.* U.S. Central Intelligence Agency:

http://www.cia.gov/nic/PDF_GIF_2020_Support/2004_05_05_papers/summary.pdf (accessed October 16, 2005).

Bert, Wayne. 2003. *The United States, China and Southeast Asian Security, A Changing of the Guard?* New York: Palgrave Macmillan.

Brawley, Mark. 2004. "The Political Economy of Balance of Power Theory," in T. V. Paul, James J. Wirtz, and Michel Fortmann (eds.), *Balance of Power: Theory and Practice in the 21st Century*. Stanford: Stanford University Press.

Chanlett-Avery, Emma. 2005. *Thailand: Background and U.S. Relations*. Congressional Research Service Report for Congress. http://fas.org/sgp/crs/row/RL32593.pdf (accessed December 06, 2006).

Chin, Kin Wah. 2004. "Singapore's perspective on the Asia-Pacific security Architecture," in See Seng Tan and Amitav Acharya (eds.), *Asia-Pacific Security Cooperation: National Interests and Regional Order*. London: M.E. Sharpe.

Chinawanno, Chulacheeb. 2002. "Thailand and Regional Security: The Search For Security Cooperation," paper presented at Conference on *Evolving Approaches to Security Cooperation in the Asia-Pacific*, Singapore: IDSS.

Chong, Ja Ian. 2004. *Testing Alternative Responses To Power Preponderance: Buffering, Binding, Bonding And Beleaguering in the Real World*. Singapore: Institute of Defence and Strategic Studies.

Dibb, Paul. 1995. *Toward a New Balance of Power in Asia*. Oxford: Oxford University Press.

Emmers, Ralf. 2001. "The Influence of the Balance of Power Factor within the ASEAN Regional Forum," *Contemporary Southeast Asia*, Vol. 23, No. 2, pp 275-91.

Far Eastern Economic Review. 1999. Eye On Asia, November 11.

Goh, Evelyn, eds. 2005. *Betwixt and Between: Southeast Asian Strategic Relations with the US and China*. Singapore: IDSS Monograph No.7.

Kuppuswamy C.S. 2006. *India's Look-East Policy: More Aggressive, Better Dividends*. South Asia Analysis Group. Paper no.1663 January 03. http://www.saag.org/%5Cpapers17%5Cpaper1663.html (accessed January 10, 2007).

Leifer, Michael. 1996. "Truth about the Balance of Power," in Da Cunha, Derek (ed.), *The Evolving Pacific Power Structure*. Singapore: Institute of Southeast Asian Studies.

Mathews, Bradley. 2003. *Bangkok's Fine Balance: Thailand's China Debate*. Hawai'i: Asia Pacific Center for Security Studies.

Nischalke, Tobias Ingo. 2000. "Insights from ASEAN's Foreign Policy Cooperation: The "ASEAN Way", a Real Spirit or Phantom?" *Contemporary Southeast Asia*, Vol. 22, No. 1, pp 89-112.

Razak, Najib T.A. 2002. *U.S.-Malaysia Defence Cooperation: A Solid Success Story*. Heritage Lecture 742, The Heritage Foundation. http://www.heritage.org/Research/AsiaandthePacific/HL742.cfm. (accessed September 12, 2003).

Ross, Robert S. 2004. "Bipolarity and Balancing in Southeast Asia" in T. V. Paul, James J. Wirtz, and Michel Fortmann (eds.), *Balance of Power: Theory and Practice in the 21st Century*. Stanford: Stanford University Press.

Roy, Denny. 2005. "Southeast Asia and China: Balancing or Bandwagoning?" *Contemporary Southeast Asia,* Vol. 27, No. 2, pp 305-23.

Schweiller, Randall. 1999. "Managing the Rise of Great Powers: History and Theory," in Alastair Iain Johnston and Robert S. Ross (eds.), *Engaging China: The Management of an Emerging Power*. London: Routledge.

World Bank. 2005. *World Development Indicators Database, 2005*. World Bank. http://www.worldbank.org/data/databytopic/GDP.pdf (accessed October 20, 2005).

CHAPTER FOUR

BEYOND THE STRAITS AND INTO THE OCEAN: IMPLICATIONS OF THE TAIWAN-CHINA RIVALRY IN THE SOUTH PACIFIC

JUSTIN B. LIANG

There is a rumor in the Marshall Islands that the abandoned Chinese Embassy building in downtown Majuro is now home to a family of *timon*, or ghosts. Bulwarked by a head-high cement barricade, the architectural anachronism, with its unmistakably Chinese red-shingled roof and majestic terra-cotta wall facings, seems surrealistically out of place, like a miniature Forbidden City transplanted thousands of miles from bustling Beijing to diminutive Delap. And since November 1998, when the Marshallese government effectively spurned China by establishing diplomatic ties with Taiwan, the forsaken structure has become emblematic of China's growing frustration over losses of its South Pacific allies to Taiwan. Indeed, as it looks to broaden its presence in Oceania, China continues to be haunted by the duplicitous diplomacy of its secession-minded island province. Within the Marshall Islands and many of its tiny island neighbors, a real-life match of *Go* is being played out between China and Taiwan, a game of diplomatic one-upmanship that exposes the friction looming latently, but impatiently, between the archrivals.

For nearly three decades, Taiwan and China have been embroiled in extraterritorial rivalries within several Pacific Island countries—countries whose geopolitical significance overshadows their comparatively miniscule land masses. Today, with the consequences of cross-strait miscalculations heightened by military modernization efforts, anti-secessionist laws by China sanctioning the use of violence against Taiwan, and increasingly vocal calls in Taipei for *de jure* independence, their struggle for dominance in the region is especially pronounced. This chapter examines the significance and implications of the Taiwan-China rivalry in the Pacific. By critically investigating the more recent diplomatic clashes, it outlines what the current interests are for both countries and relates the implications of their conflicting interests for China, for Taiwan, for the Pacific Island countries involved, and for the region as a whole. It argues that while a shift in the regional balance of power is certainly a conceivable consequence of the Taiwan-China rivalry in Oceania, it is but a distant one; a more pressing and immediate concern is the possibility of heightened regional instability actuated by the impulsive and often misinformed diplomatic decisions of island statesmen, who appear increasingly willing to buy into the corruptive checkbook politics of both countries. Ultimately, the current stakes are highest not for the bigger players—China, Taiwan, the United States, Australia, and Japan—but for the vulnerable island nations themselves, who have both the most to gain and the most to lose from their diplomatic engagements with the "two Chinas."

China: Current Interests and Implications

China's current interests in Oceania appear to be borne from a "big picture" strategy favoring long-term objectives over immediate gain. From a geographic perspective, the vast maritime expanse of the region could serve a prudent strategic purpose: control of regional resources could greatly expand the country's sphere of influence, and both the land and water could potentially be used for grander military pursuits, for example surveillance, weapons testing, and naval operations. Though the Chinese have continually denied allegations of military interest within the islands—beginning with their eagerness to sign the South Pacific Nuclear Free Zone Treaty in 1987 and repeated public avowals by Chinese foreign affairs officials defending their benevolent motives[1]—a catalogue of activities over the past decade suggests otherwise.

The first involves the construction of a satellite tracking station on Kiribati's South Tarawa Island by China in 1997. Though China maintained that the station, one of three of such installations overseas, was purely benign and lacked surveillance capabilities,[2] others—including

[1] In a statement made in response to China's donation of military supplies to Fiji in late 1998, China's ambassador to Fiji, Zhang Junsai, responded, "We promote defense ties as part of friendly relations. Look at our history in the region. You cannot find any strategic purpose in the activities of China." See Elizabeth Feizkhah, "Making Friends," *Asiaweek* (June 15, 2001).

[2] Chinese authorities reported, rather, that the facility was used to track Chinese space vehicles and even played a role in China's first manned space mission. See

Kiribati's President, Anote Tong[3]—believed it may have been a clandestine "spy post," used, perhaps, to view U.S. missile testing operations in the Marshall Islands. But whether it was or not, the tracking system illuminated the potential for abuse of the islands as military terrain. The ease with which China transacted the lease of the Tarawa land, which conveniently hugs the equator—an "ideal zone for launching rockets and 'parking' satellites in orbit" (Feizkhah 2001)—exposed Kiribati's soft spot for "duty-free" money. Moreover, the abrupt shutdown of the station in November 2003, when Kiribati unexpectedly flip-flopped allegiances to Taiwan, and the fiery protests that ensued,[4] strongly hinted that China had something to hide within the confines of the now-defunct facility.

Recent military gifts to the armed forces of Melanesian countries also seem to implicate China's military objectives in the region. Between 1995 and 1998, China donated over US$500,000—in the form of uniforms, tents, gym equipment and even martial arts training—each to Tonga, Fiji, Papua New Guinea, and Vanuatu. Frequent visits to these countries by Chinese military delegations provide further evidence that China's motives may have significant strategic underpinnings. In February 1998, the Chinese Minister of Defense at the time, Chi Haotian, visited the Fiji government with a 13-member delegation and met with Brigadier-General Ratu Epeli Ganilau, the Commander of Fiji's military forces to discuss "common interests" ("Chinese Defense Minister Visiting Fiji" 1998). In November 2000, at the South Pacific Forum Meeting in Kiribati, West Papuan separatist leaders made contact with Chinese officials and were later flown to Beijing to meet with Chinese bureaucratic elites, purportedly to marshal support in their struggle for independence (Bohane 2001a). In

---

Melody Chen, "Feelings mixed over Kiribati ties," *Taipei Times* (November 9, 2003: 1).

[3] During his 2003 speech in the Kiribati presidential elections, opposition candidate Anote Tong often alluded to the secrecy surrounding China's facility. The suspicions he aroused were reported to have won him major support. See "Kiribati prepares for backlash after recognizing Taiwan," *ABC News Online* (November 10, 2003), http://www.abc.net.au/news/newsitems/200311/s984911.htm, and Hamish McDonald, "Tiny Pacific islands play China using the Taiwan card," *The Age* (November 10, 2003), http://www.theage.com.au/articles/2003/11/09/1068329419844.html

[4] China's then-ambassador to Kiribati, Ma Shuxue, denounced Kiribati's sudden switch as a "gross violation of the 'one China' principle." The Chinese were also believed to have instigated protests outside parliament opposing the government's rapid decision. See Graham Norris, "Pawns in the Game: Pacific Becoming Key Battleground Between Taiwan and China," *Pacific Magazine* (March 2005), http://www.pacificislands.cc/pm52004/pmdefault.php?urlarticleid=0001

May 2001, a Chinese military delegation flew to Port Moresby in an apparent attempt to "woo PNG defense forces" (Bohane 2001b). And in July 2007, Fiji's Ministry of Foreign Affairs established a new military-diplomatic post in China, sending Major Neumi Leweni to Beijing to serve as Fiji's first "defense attaché" to the country. With bans on official military ties with both Australia and New Zealand, Fiji has repeatedly proclaimed its readiness to enhance military-to-military relations with China (Field 2007).

Such gestures paint a telling, if somewhat blurry, portrait of China's strategic aims in the region. Beijing's courtship of these countries—particularly in Melanesia, where defense forces already exist—underscores the country's interest in establishing a military footprint therein. The Chinese military may be seeking use of the Pacific Island chains as "access points" for logistical re-supply, maintenance, or relief from operational deployment (Kamphausen and Liang 2007). Military collaboration may also foreshadow China's desire to develop expansive blue water navy, which it currently lacks, in the South Pacific.

Meanwhile, the West Papua episode raised eyebrows about China's political influence in the region, alarming the *de facto* "peace brokers" of the area, Australia and New Zealand, who recognize Indonesian sovereignty over West Papua and remain concerned about the possibility of a violent secessionist movement within the territory.[5] The incident in Tarawa, moreover, demonstrated that China is surprisingly undaunted in its pursuit of strategic operations within these countries. As Ben Reilly and John Henderson have rightly concluded,

> "Whatever the real purpose of the space-tracking station, the fact that China operates a military facility on the territory of a Pacific Island Forum member stands as a reminder that the potential strategic significance of the Pacific islands may be exploited by non-Western powers" (Henderson and Reilly 2003).

While there is less at stake economically for China, it does nevertheless hope to harvest some fiscal fruits given its lengthy record of investment—mostly in the form of untraced aid, funneled through the newly launched China-South Pacific Cooperation Fund—in many of the

---

[5] Franzalbert Joku, the "International Moderator" for the West Papuan Presidium Council, stated to the press after meeting with Chinese diplomats that West Papuans would give "first option" in diplomatic recognition, and Taiwan second. See Ben Bohane, "Papuans' nod to China leaves Canberra in a quandary," *Sydney Morning Herald* (May 29, 2001: 12).

countries, and particularly in Melanesia.[6] China's commercial presence, stretching from West Papua to Fiji, has expanded dramatically over the past 10 years, with countries like Fiji and Papua New Guinea now exporting large portions of their top commodities, like timber, to China.[7] The recent surge of investment in plantations and garment factories also evince China's profit-seeking motives, as does the recent opening of a Pacific Trade Office in Beijing. Marine and mineral resources in the Pacific have been of interest to China since its trading days with Fiji and Western Samoa in the early 19th century (Yee 1976), and the country's ongoing hunt for raw materials to support its meteoric economic growth has driven a number of expensive resource extraction projects throughout the Pacific—including the multibillion dollar, majority Chinese-owned Ramu nickel mine in Papua New Guinea's Madang province.

Yet, beyond diplomatic competition with Taiwan for votes in international bodies like the United Nations, speculative military strategies, and dubious economic prospects, what is China's actual goal? Most plausibly, China's engagement in the Pacific is part of its longer-term hegemonic ambitions. An alliance of friendly client states in the region, not unlike the one China has been cultivating in Southeast Asia, would certainly be of strategic utility should regional tensions warrant the use of force or intervention beyond China's borders. Now is an ideal time for China to capitalize on the languishing grip of the United States on the region and forge what could, in time, be invaluable overseas bonds. Realistically, given its growing list of more crucial foreign policy concerns right now—including an ebbing relationship with Japan—China's diplomacy in the region has much less to do with a genuine sympathy for these developing countries than with the geostrategic dimensions of its global "grand strategy."

Taiwan: Current Interests and Implications

Taiwan's interests in Oceania seem more immediate, and stem from its separatist leanings and politically motivated desire for legitimacy and recognition as an independent nation. Six of the 26 countries with which Taiwan has established official diplomatic relations are situated in the

---

[6] This bias can likely be explained by Melanesia's having greater mineral and forestry resources than Micronesia or Polynesia, however poorly managed in the past.

[7] For more specific economic figures, see Kalinga Seneviratne, "Australia uneasy as Beijing woos South Pacific," *Asia Times* (August 16, 2000), http://archives.pireport.org/archive/2001/august/08%2D16%2D04.htm

Pacific—political non-entities, had they not the representative voting power of much larger countries in major international bodies such as the United Nations. In its ongoing scramble for membership in such organizations, Taiwan needs all the support it can get—even the backing of a country with fewer than 70,000 total residents, like the Marshall Islands. For recognition purposes, a vote from microscopic Tuvalu is arguably as good as one from Australia.

A recent incident involving Taiwan's bid to gain observer status at the World Health Assembly (WHA), the governing body of the World Health Organization (WHO), attests to this drive. At the WHA's 58th conference in Geneva in May 2005, Taiwan failed to win a majority of votes that would have granted it observer status with the Assembly—a precursor to membership in the WHO. Of the 21 affirmative votes, several came from Pacific Island countries, including Papua New Guinea, the Solomon Islands, and Fiji. What is interesting to note is that the Taiwan President himself, Chen Shui-Bian, personally visited these countries just weeks prior to the conference—in spite of their diplomatic ties with China—ostensibly to garner support for this cause ("Health Minister Rapped Over Taiwan Support" 2005).

The failed bid proved that Taiwan has a long way to go before its Pacific support base nets any meaningful political clout. Yet, a more striking aftereffect of the vote was the diplomatic row that percolated between China, Papua New Guinea, the Solomon Islands, and Fiji over the last three's support of Taiwan. Such duplicity suggests that diplomatically indecisive island countries do not feel the need to play by the "rules" of the Taiwan-China game, and that their ambivalent foreign policy remains amenable to ulterior incentives. To be fair, though, one could just as easily argue that such pretenses are merely natural responses to the false promises of Taiwan and China, whose hands in the diplomatic tug-of-war are equally as shifty.

In addition to these political aims, Taiwan appears intent on sustaining its vested economic endeavors in the region, as its South Pacific fishing fleets represent one of Taiwan's largest commercial projects abroad ("Joint Statement" 2000). Diplomatic partnerships facilitate the consignment of requisite fishing licenses and ensure that the economic rewards continued to be reaped. Tuna in the Pacific, it seems, has made Taiwan a major player in the global fisheries industry, and the loss of legal rights to the ocean could have sizeable economic consequences—at least 300 million NT dollars a year—for Taiwan.

Current trends do not seem to favor Taiwan's economic and political motives. While generous and arguably more creative in its aid distribution than China—funding humanitarian projects like the PNG Red Cross, technical missions, and a successful scholarship program—Taiwan continues to play second fiddle as a diplomatic option, likely because it lacks the funding firepower of its mainland counterpart. Not surprisingly, the six Pacific Island countries with which it currently maintains ties—Nauru, the Marshall Islands, Kiribati, Palau, Tuvalu, and the Solomon Islands—are among the smallest and most resource deprived in the region, with comparatively limited development potential. And Taiwan's worsening record of bribery and exploitation in the islands, discussed in the final section of this chapter, bode ominously for its political prospects—both abroad and at home. In 2004, allegations of a bribery scandal between the Taiwan Foreign Ministry and Vanuatu's Prime Minister Serge Vohor made front-page headlines in several Chinese and Taiwanese newspapers. Because the affair coincided with the Taiwan parliamentary elections, the incumbent government was reproached for corruption in what became a "world-wide media blitz" (Neil-Jones 2004b).

Pacific Island Countries: Interests and Implications

Clashes between Taiwan and China have figured most prominently in seven countries—the Marshall Islands, Kiribati, Tonga, the Solomon Islands, Papua New Guinea, Vanuatu, and Nauru—all of which have in recent times wavered in their diplomatic allegiances. News reports about these often capricious diplomatic switches tell virtually identical stories: Forum Island Country X signs joint communiqué with China/Taiwan, infuriates ex-benefactor, and triggers unrelenting accusations of foul play (and other forms of wrath). To an extent, however, such patterns are becoming increasingly predictable: they result from the *sub-rosa* outbidding of financial assistance by one country over the other and include a side smattering of provisory negotiations, usually during or immediately after a lavish junket taken by island leaders to the donor country—an unethical but effective combination of "dollar diplomacy" and what some have termed "visit diplomacy."

There is little doubt that money principally drives the diplomatic decisions of island leaders, and a growing body of evidence that implicates both Taiwan and China in exploiting this tendency and engaging in economic foul play. In December 2004, former Prime Minister of Vanuatu Edward Natapei proclaimed that he was offered US$2 million by a third-party lawyer to establish diplomatic ties with Taiwan. According to Natapei, "It was all strictly on a top-secret basis. We were also offered free trips to Taiwan. I told the Council of Ministers what had happened and the idea of diplomatic ties with Taiwan was rejected out of hand" (Neil-Jones 2004a). A similar story emerged from Kiribati in 2003, when allegations spread that linked newly elected President Anote Tong to a bribery scandal with Taiwan. In April 2005, the *Marshall Islands Journal* confirmed sources claiming that government officials were accepting *payolas* from the Chinese to re-establish relations with China:

> "Sources alleged that people linked to China made payments to many United Democratic Party elected leaders and other party members beginning last December. . . . The payments reportedly amounted to between US$6,000 and US$10,000 to senators and Cabinet ministers and were made to encourage a return of diplomatic ties with China" ("Chinese Bribe Scandal Hits Marshalls" 2005).

Most recently, in 2006, Taiwan brazenly intervened in the Solomon Islands' parliamentary elections by backing a number of pro-Taiwan candidates with funds distributed through questionable channels.[8] The elections brought forth a slew of accusations from the opposition Labor Party, whose president, Joses Tuhanuku, publicly stated that,

> "a clear connection exists between the payment of monies by Taiwan and various political maneuverings by the Prime Minister. What it amounts to is that Taiwan is running a shadow aid program that is being used to corrupt our political processes and the prime minister is fully colluding with them" (Tuhanuku 2006).

Not surprisingly, however, Beijing also played a gambit in the elections, allegedly setting up a secret US$1.2 million "slush fund" with a former opposition leader to support politicians who promised to sever the country's diplomatic ties with Taiwan (Squires 2006).

Bribe money, like "official" Chinese and Taiwanese largesse, comes with no strings attached; and though accusations and, in some instances, proof of such dealings have emerged, no one has to date been convicted. Both China and Taiwan appear unhesitant to take advantage of these

---

[8] According to an Australian Broadcasting Corporation radio report after the riots, some protesters claimed that the newly elected PM and his coalition government were funded and manipulated by the owner of the Honiara Hotel, Sir Thomas Chan, a naturalized Solomon Islands' citizen of Chinese origin. See "Taiwan diplomacy linked to Solomons' unrest," *The World Today*, Australian Broadcasting Corporation Radio National (Sydney, Australia: ABC, April 20, 2006).

countries' lack of government accountability, and this audacity—coupled with the continued willingness of government officials to accept such bribes—has fuelled and perpetuated the exploitation.

The continued collusion of Pacific Island leaders with Taiwanese and Chinese diplomats invites an important question about how such behavior, executed at the individual level, affects interests at the state level. To wit, what are the implications of these diplomatic decisions for the island nations themselves? It is suggested here that both the political and economic ramifications of playing "checkbook politics" with China and Taiwan are potentially much greater than island statesmen may believe—and certainly much graver for these countries, at least in the immediate future, than for either China or Taiwan.

Many island countries still believe that allegiance swapping is an innocuous practice, incurring few costs relative to economic gains. While an argument can certainly be made for the economic windfalls of these often transient relationships, such fickle foreign policy may in turn promote regional instability by upsetting the balance of regional economic partners—specifically, by influencing the way subsequent offers of aid are furnished by other regional actors, from Australia to the World Bank—and by impinging upon the independence of these already politically and economically fragile nation states. These high-stakes contingencies are most clearly exemplified in two recent episodes: one in Vanuatu and the other in the Solomon Islands.

In November 2004, Vanuatu's then-Prime Minister Serge Vohor found himself—and his country—mired in a tense political impasse after making false promises to both China and Taiwan. In October, after being wined and dined in Beijing courtesy of the Chinese government, Vohor pledged diplomatic allegiance to China, firmly decreeing his adherence to the "one China" policy in exchange for over VT320 million (US$3 million) in unrestricted aid. Then, in a seemingly bipolar betrayal, Vohor flew secretly to Taipei on November 3, where he proceeded—without the knowledge or consent of his foreign ministry—to establish a diplomatic pact with Taiwan, promising to support Taiwan's bid to join organizations such as the United Nations after being conferred an undisclosed amount of cash and an offer of "genuine development assistance," according to a Taiwanese Foreign Affairs official (Banham and Skehan 2004).

Whether it was Vohor's aim to reap remuneration from both China and Taiwan, an upshot of bribery, or a foolish belief that he could somehow maintain relations with both, the consequences were severe. The Parliamentary cabinet issued a no-confidence vote that impeached Vohor and rapidly installed a new Prime Minister, Ham Lini. Not surprisingly, one of Lini's first engagements as PM was a trip to Beijing, reaffirming Vanuatu's bilateral ties to China and apologizing for his predecessor's perfidy. Another more significant outcome was a November 25, 2004, statement by Australian Foreign Minister Alexander Downer threatening to cut a third of its AU$31 million aid program to Vanuatu should the Vohor government continue to abuse its power (Gaglioti 2004). Vohor's impetuous diplomatic decisions nearly alienated the country's largest aid donor, Australia; and had Vohor not been expelled from office, the economic repercussions from the Chinese and Australian aid fallout would have been disastrous. In effect, the Taiwan-China issue had a destabilizing effect on the entire nation, foregrounding the corruptibility of the incumbent government and exposing its powerlessness at the hands of its affluent Northeast Asian suitors.[9]

A similar series of events transpired in the Solomon Islands in 2000, when Prime Minister Massaneh Sogavare mistakenly presumed he could extort aid money from both China and Taiwan simultaneously. Though the Solomons recognized Taiwan as a diplomatic partner, Sogavare and his Foreign Affairs Minister, Danny Philip, made frequent trips to Beijing without the approval of the Cabinet—apparently in an attempt to salvage, with the help of Chinese funds, its collapsing export base, and an economy that had contracted 14% in real terms over the course of the year ("Solomon Islands Foreign Minister Must Answer for Beijing Trip" 2000). These events played a role in Australia's subsequent truncation of aid to the Solomons, with Australian Foreign Minister Alexander Downer demanding that the Sogavare government "return to Western-supervised fiscal austerity" before assistance be resumed (Byrne 2001). Australia also suggested that other aid donors, including the World Bank and the International Monetary Fund, do likewise.

This charade, like Vohor's gaffe in Vanuatu, divulged the country's dire need for greater transparency at all levels—among elites atop the bureaucracy as well as between elites and the masses. It also demonstrated how greedy government officials put their entire country at risk, both economically and politically, by misguided foreign policy decisions. While the amounts of money at play might be small for Taiwan and China, they are hardly insignificant to recipient countries whose GDPs are but a

---

[9] Also worthy of mention here is a 2001 incident in Vanuatu in which deposed Prime Minister Barak Sope sought to play the China card after Australia and New Zealand chided the Sope administration for corrupt foreign policy practices. Sope's ties to China were likely instrumental in Vohor's recent power play with both China and Taiwan. See Bill Standish, "China in the Pacific," *Sydney Morning Herald* (May 28, 2001: 12).

fraction of their benefactors'. In 1999 in Papua New Guinea, for example, Prime Minister Bill Skate forfeited over US$100 million in aid from China after swapping ties to Taiwan, which had reportedly agreed to provide the country with soft loans as high as US$4 billion (McKew 1999). In 2002, all-but-bankrupt Nauru went further in debt after jumping ship to China. Taiwan nearly pursued legal action to force payment on an outstanding US$12.5 million loan it granted to the impoverished country to build a luxury hotel.[10]

To this effect, Taiwan-China "checkbook diplomacy" becomes a divisive and critical issue, feeding the corruption of money-hungry government officials and encouraging an unhealthy reliance on financial assistance. Should impoverished island countries continue to seek bail-out money from China and Taiwan—and should China and Taiwan continue to accede—there is a danger of developing a helpless dependency on unrestricted aid. And by estranging other donor countries and institutions in the process, these countries also run the risk of becoming mere puppets to their much stronger patrons—a cancerous unilateral relationship that could over time undermine their very sovereignty.

Conclusions: Regional and Global Implications of the Taiwan-China Rivalry

Bribery and poor governance are costing many island countries their critical revenue-generating resources, as players like China and Taiwan are keen to exploit these countries' comparative disadvantages in the commercial sector. Illicit Chinese and Taiwanese activities in the Pacific are nowhere more pronounced than in the fisheries industry, where over US$2 billion is grossed annually. Taiwan has 62 total fishing vessels in the Pacific, and its new fleet of "jumbo" super-seiners, which can haul in an unprecedented 20,000 tons of tuna per year, has recently upset the governing Forum Fisheries Agency (FFA).[11] Taiwan in particular has a poor track record of maritime integrity, being charged with misdemeanors ranging from over-fishing in Palau to breaching the Exclusive Economic Zones in Fiji—creating what some have called a "black hole for fish products" (Whitney 2005). The fisheries industry offers a sobering indicator that the promises of "mutual cooperation" so commonly

---

[10] Not surprisingly, China, in the end, bailed out the country.

[11] Fiji has already banned the use of these seiners. See "Increasing numbers of 'jumbo' boats threaten tuna resources," *Tahiti Press* (June 18, 2004), http://archives.pireport.org/archive/2004/june/06%2D18%2D03.htm

trumpeted by sweet-talking Chinese and Taiwanese diplomats are often insincere. There is an urgent need to improve accountability within the bureaucracy, to prosecute those responsible, and to re-focus on promoting more meaningful projects with aid money—such as agricultural missions and trade assistance, which require real bilateral cooperation and provide sustainable social and economic benefits.

At the societal level, the China-Taiwan rivalry is also agitating the pot of volatile ethnic tensions already bubbling in many of these countries. After the 2006 ministerial elections in the Solomon Islands, for example, massive riots broke out in the capital, and much of Honiara's Chinatown was burned and looted. The violence—the country's worst since 2003—appeared to stem from public resentment over Taiwan's "dirty" influence in the elections, and from a billowing undercurrent of ethnic unrest among the Chinese and locals, who see the former as dominating the islands' business and politics. A similar, though less serious riot erupted in the Tongan capital of Nuku'alofa in November 2006, when violent hooligans ransacked over 30 Chinese stores and businesses.

These incidents resonate with an emerging trend in the Pacific regarded by many to be an ominous harbinger of future social instability. As Chinese and Taiwanese diasporas expand in the Pacific, and as Chinese businesses continue to reap financial success at the expense of local ones, the social and economic repercussions of Chinese and Taiwanese penetration into these islands' fragile economies become increasingly salient. Both parties must be especially careful not to compete in a way that upsets traditional economic patterns or marginalizes local methods of doing business.

Another important corollary is that major regional players like Australia are fast losing their appeal, seeing their economic leverage dwindle in the face of their increasingly generous Northeast Asian counterparts. In September 2003, PNG Prime Minister Michael Somare was "fuming" over a letter from Australian PM John Howard suggesting more Australians be placed in key strategic decision making positions in PNG to curb corruption ("Somare angry over Howard's letter" 2003). Senior officials in the Prime Minister's Office then insinuated that they would rather bring in technical experts from East Asia than take Australia's advice, later demonizing AusAID as a "big middle-man" who handled all the aid money. PNG's ex-Prime Minister Bill Skate shared Somare's sentiments about its regional "big brother," telling the country to "mind its own business" in July 1999 after Australia denounced an impromptu visit by Skate to Taipei to seek Taiwanese funds ("PNG Tells Australia to Mind its Own Business" 1999). Chinese aid to PNG is now a close second to that of Australia, and if the trend continues, China could very well sit atop that list within the next decade.

For aid-giving institutions such as the World Bank, the feeling of distrust is becoming more mutual. For example, in 2005 the Bank withdrew from a US$34.3 million loan agreement to Papua New Guinea's Forestry and Conservation Project after timber companies failed to comply with harvest requirements and meet provisional social obligations to landowners ("Forest protection program dumped" 2005). A recent World Bank study indicated that governance in Melanesian countries has worsened over the past six years, based on a series of indicators gauging accountability, government effectiveness, and control of corruption, among other things (World Bank 2001). The Taiwan-China rivalry certainly factored into the World Bank's equation, what with all the domestic scandals—especially in PNG, the Solomons, and Vanuatu—it provoked.

In the long term, both China and Taiwan—but particularly the former—will likely represent key players in the region, both economically and in terms of leadership. But an answer to what will ultimately become of the region's tectonic relationships is inextricably tied to a set of hypothetical "if-then" statements. If the United States continues to neglect China's Pacific strategy, for example, China may well continue to carve out a broad sphere of influence throughout the Pacific, maintaining use of the islands as strategic "access points," deepening military cooperation, and extracting whatever resources it can from its growing palate of business ventures. On the other hand, if China and Taiwan somehow reach accord on the "one China" policy, their entire South Pacific rivalry would be rendered largely inconsequential. Regional dynamics—the economic, political, and security landscape of the South Pacific—would be subject to an entirely new set of variables. And if China suddenly begins to feel that the costs associated with Pacific islands' whim-like diplomacy are too asymmetric, mitigating any strategic benefit the country may derive from its regional investments, perhaps the issue may fizzle to relative unimportance.

What can be inferred from recent events, however, is that Pacific islands involved in this standoff must proceed with utmost caution. While each party is expected to maintain its own agenda in the aid game—for the islands, access to readily available, untied sums of money; for Taiwan, the hope of greater international recognition; and for China, the chance to project power in a strategically favorable location—it is incumbent upon island nations to recognize the consequences of accepting such funds without the proper conditions. For this real-life match of *Go* is only a two-player game, and the spaces on the game board—that is, the island nations themselves—are really the ones being played.

Works Cited

Banham, Cynthia and Craig Skehan. November 27, 2004. "High-stakes diplomacy in Vanuatu," *Port Vila Presse.*

Biddick, Thomas V. 1989. "Diplomatic Rivalry in the South Pacific: The PRC and Taiwan," *Asian Survey*, vol. 29, no. 8, August 1989, pp 800-815.

Bohane, Ben. 2001a. "West Papuans seek Beijing's support," *Sydney Morning Herald*. May 18, 2001: A12.

—. 2001. "Papuans' nod to China leaves Canberra in a quandary," *Sydney Morning Herald*. May 29, 2001: 12.

Byrne, Peter. 2001 "Solomon Islands government fighting for survival," *World Socialist Web Site*. (June 30, 2001). http://www.wsws.org/articles/2001/jun2001/solo-j30.shtml (accessed February 22, 2005).

Chen, Melody. 2003. "Feelings mixed over Kiribati ties," *Taipei Times* (November 9, 2003).

"China Bribe Scandal Hits Marshalls," *Marshall Islands Journal* (April 30, 2005). http://www.taipeitimes.com/News/taiwan/archives/2005/04/30/2003252555 (accessed March 1, 2005).

"Chinese Defense Minister Visiting Fiji," *Pacific News* (February 10, 1998). http://archives.pireport.org/archive/1998/february/02%2D10%2D08.html (accessed February 22, 2005).

Dorney, Sean. "China 'Serious' About Taiwan's Involvement in Pacific Islands Forum," *Radio Australia* (November 2, 2000). http://166.122.164.43/archive/2000/November/11-02-02.htm (accessed March 2, 2005).

Feizkhah, Elizabeth. 2001. "Making Friends: Beijing is courting the island nations in the Pacific. Is it just extending a helping hand, trying to isolate archrival Taiwan—or getting ready to confront the U.S.?" *Asiaweek* (June 15, 2001).

Field, Michael. 2007. "Prominent Fiji Military Man Heading to China," *Stuff.co.nz* (July 11, 2007). http://www.stuff.co.nz/4123174a6160.html#Scene_1.

"Forest protection program dumped," *Papua New Guinea Post-Courier Online* (May 20, 2005).

http://www.postcourier.com.pg/20050520/news03.htm (accessed May 21, 2005).

"Forum Strengthens Statement on West Papua," *Radio Australia* (October 31, 2000). http://166.122.164.43/archive/2000/October/10-31-05.htm (accessed March 17, 2005).

Gaglioti, Frank. 2004. "Vanuatu government collapses following Australian economic threats," *World Socialist Web Site* (December 22, 2004). http://www.wsws.org/articles/2004/dec2004/vanu-d22.shtml (accessed March 4, 2005).

"Health Minister Rapped Over Taiwan Support," *Pacific Daily News* (May 20, 2005). http://www.pacificislands.cc/pina/pinadefault2.php?urlpinaid=15452 (accessed May 21, 2005).

Henderson, John and Benjamin Reilly. 2003. "Dragon in Paradise: China's Rising Star in Oceania," *The National Interest*, Summer 2003, pp 94-104.

"Increasing numbers of 'jumbo' boats threaten tuna resources," *Tahiti Press* (June 18, 2004). http://archives.pireport.org/archive/2004/june/06%2D18%2D03.htm (accessed May 1, 2005).

Johnson, Giff. 2004. "Taiwan Firm on Anti-Missile Referendum," *Marianas Variety* (January 14, 2004).

—. 2003. "Tiny Kiribati Puts Dent in China's Armor," *Marianas Variety* (November 18, 2003). http://archives.pireport.org/archive/2003/november/11%2D18%2D03.htm (accessed March 23, 2005).

"Joint Statement, Eighth Taiwan/Republic of China-Forum Countries Dialogue (Tarawa, Kiribati)," (November 1, 2000). http://www.forumsec.org.fj/news/2000/Nov01.htm (accessed May 15, 2005).

Kamphausen, Roy D. and Justin Liang. 2007. "PLA Power Projection: Current Realities and Emerging Trends," in Michael Swaine et al. (eds.), *Assessing the Threat: The Chinese Military and Taiwan Security*. Washington, DC: Carnegie Endowment for International Peace, 2007.

"Kiribati prepares for backlash after recognising Taiwan," *ABC News Online*. (November 10, 2003). http://www.abc.net.au/news/newsitems/200311/s984911.htm (accessed March 1, 2005).

Lintner, Bertil. 2004. "Diplomacy: A New Battle for the Pacific," *Far Eastern Economic Review* (August 5, 2004).

http://www.asiapacificms.com/articles/china_pacific/ (accessed May 15, 2005).

McDonald, Hamish. 2003. "Tiny Pacific islands play China using the Taiwan card," *The Age* (November 10, 2003). http://www.theage.com.au/articles/2003/11/09/1068329419844.html (accessed May 1, 2005).

Neil-Jones, Marc. 2004a. "Natapei was offered $2 million to recognize Taiwan," *Port Vila Presse* (December 8, 2004).

—. 2004b. "Vanuatu Charade Saves Taiwan Elections," *Vanuatu Daily Post* (December 14, 2004). http://archives.pireport.org/archive/2004/december/12%2D14%2Dcom.htm (accessed May 15, 2005).

Norris, Graham. 2005. "Pawns in the Game: Pacific Becoming Key Battleground Between Taiwan and China," *Pacific Magazine* (March 2005). http://www.pacificislands.cc/pm52004/pmdefault.php?urlarticleid=0001 (accessed March 1, 2005).

"PNG tells Australia to mind its own business," *Pacific Islands Report* (July 5, 1999). http://archives.pireport.org/archive/1999/july/07%2D06%2D01.html (accessed May 3, 2005).

"Possible Diplomatic Row Looming Between Fiji and China," *Pacific Daily News* (May 17, 2005). http://www.pacificislands.cc/pina/pinadefault2.php?urlpinaid=15401 (accessed May 18, 2005).

Seneviratne, Kalinga. 2000. "Australia uneasy as Beijing woos South Pacific," *Asia Times* (August 16, 2000). http://archives.pireport.org/archive/2001/august/08%2D16%2D04.htm (accessed May 15, 2005).

Sinutuli, Lopeti. 1997. "The Impact of Asia in Pacific Today," *Asia Pacific Newsletter* (Osaka), no. 10 (August 1997). http://www.hurights.or.jp/asia-pacific/no_10/no10_impact.htm (accessed May 18, 2005).

"Solomon Islands Foreign Minister Must Answer for Beijing Trip," *PINA Nius Online* (October 12, 2000). http://archives.pireport.org/archive/2000/october/10%2D12%2Dup1.htm (accessed May 3, 2005).

"Somare angry over Howard's letter," *The National* (Papua New Guinea) (September 1, 2003). http://archives.pireport.org/archive/2003/september/09%2D01%2D04.htm (accessed May 16, 2005).

Squires, Nick. 2005. "Pacific Persuasion: Beijing's increasing economic muscle in the South Pacific," *South China Morning Post* (July 21, 2005).

Standish, Bill. 2001. "China in the Pacific," *Sydney Morning Herald* (May 28, 2001): 12.

"Taiwan diplomacy linked to Solomons' unrest," *The World Today*. Australian Broadcasting Corporation Radio National (April 20, 2006). http://www.abc.net.au/worldtoday/content/2006/s1619951.htm (accessed August 10, 2007).

Tuhanuku, Joses. 2006. *Labour leader urges voters not to support corrupt candidates*, Press Release, Solomon Islands Labour Party, Honiara, March 2006.

"Vohor Embraces China in Surprise Switch" *Radio Australia* (November 4, 2004). http://archives.pireport.org/archive/2004/november/11%2D04%2D02.htm (accessed April 20, 2005).

Whitney, Scott. 2005. "Fish Wars: Pacific Fisheries Face Biological and Economic Woes," *Pacific Magazine* (May 2005). http://www.pacificislands.cc/pm22004/pmdefault.php?urlarticleid=0030 (accessed May 18, 2005).

World Bank. 2001. *The World Bank, Structural Adjustments, and Melanesia* (December 1, 2001). http://www.melanesia.org/2001AAA/worldbank.htm (accessed May 15, 2005).

Yee, Sin Joan. 1976 *The Chinese in the Pacific*. Fiji: South Pacific Social Sciences Association.

Part III

The Emerging Volatility

CHAPTER FIVE

IS ECONOMICS "MISSING THE POINT" ON LAND? COMMODIFICATION OF LAND AND IMPACT OF NON-INDIGENOUS CONCEPTS OF LAND IN BOUGAINVILLE

ANTHEA MOORE

Concepts of "land" held by many indigenous peoples are fundamentally different to Western concepts of land. In particular, the Western conceptualization and use of land as a *commodity* is largely incompatible with the concept of land as *identity* that is held by indigenous Melanesians and many other indigenous peoples. This is important because the commodification of land is widely considered to be a precondition of economic development. In Bougainville, conflicting concepts of land were transformed into violent conflict when they were combined with other tensions and grievances related to the Panguna mine. The absence of a strong state was critical to this conflict evolving from conceptual to physical.

Where concepts of land held by indigenous peoples are similarly incompatible with Western concepts, violent conflicts can be expected to recur in Papua New Guinea (PNG) and other weak states in Melanesia and worldwide. Where states are strong enough to suppress violent conflict, the conceptual conflict will still persist and is likely to manifest in other ways. By acknowledging and explicitly addressing this conceptual conflict between land as a commodity and land as identity, solutions may be found that allow these concepts to be reconciled in a way that minimizes the damage done to the quality of economic property rights and also to the social fabric of indigenous communities.

In this chapter I begin by examining what indigenous Melanesian and Bougainvillean concepts of land were prior to Western contact and what they currently are. I compare these to Western concepts of land, in particular the economic concept of land as a commodity. I then outline the role of land in the Bougainville crisis to demonstrate the very real implications of the conflict between these two concepts of land. Examining how economics has attempted to accommodate indigenous concepts of land in order to facilitate economic development, I propose that these attempts are currently inadequate and are likely to remain so. Finally, I consider the future prospects for economic development in Bougainville and other places where indigenous concepts of land are in conflict with Western concepts.

Concepts of Land

As was the case throughout most of Melanesia, the indigenous, pre-colonial concepts of land in Bougainville are understood to have been complex, multifaceted and integral to the identity of Bougainvillean peoples. Land was not only a vital supplier of life and livelihood, but also had spiritual, cultural and social significance. Land rights were also bound up with individual's relationships to one another. For Melanesians "(l)and cannot be 'just' land" because it has social and cultural contexts and just as kinship binds people to people, the people are bound to their land," (Ballard 1997).

In 1974, three Bougainvillean students described the role of land as

> "our physical life (and) our social life; it is marriage; it is status; it is security; it is politics; in fact, it is our only world … We have little or no experience of social survival detached from the land. For us to be completely landless is a nightmare which no dollar in the pocket or dollar in the bank will allay; we are a threatened people" (Dove, Miriung and Togolo 1974).

Although written after a significant period of Western contact, this description reflects the multiple roles that land had, and continues to have, in the lives of Bougainvilleans and other Melanesians. Importantly, it also foreshadows the uncertainty and social disruption likely to result from landlessness.

In contrast to much of Melanesia, primary land ownership rights in Bougainville are most commonly passed through the female line. While males may have the right to "speak" for the land, these speaking rights are conferred by relationships to female landowners who can also veto any decision regarding land (Saovana-Spriggs 2003). There are typically several overlying overlapping land usage rights of various types held simultaneously over any particular area of land. Where, for example, hunting rights could be held by a male relative, while the garden is more closely controlled by the female owner. Concepts of land vary between Bougainville and other part of Melanesia, and there are also differences between regions of Bougainville, and between clans. Ultimately the meaning of land to one person can never be identical to that of any other person.

Despite the inherent difficulty in trying to delineate exactly what "land" means to Bougainvilleans, it is evident that there is a special relationship that is fundamentally different to the Western relationship to land. Chris Ballard succinctly explains that although the relationship to land that is claimed by many Melanesians varies and is inherently difficult to define, it is "manifest in a particularly resilient form of attachment to land, and that these ties are not seen to diminish swiftly over time" (Ballard 1997).

In present day Bougainville, concepts of land must necessarily be different from what they were prior to contact with Westerners. Western education, religion, the apparatus of the state, commercial agriculture, Panguna and other mines, compensation payments and a decade of violence, are all part of the experience of being a modern Bougainvillean and all have implications for how land is conceptualized. An additional layer of complication and confusion has been added by the separatist movement that became a focus of the Bougainville Liberation Army from the late 1980's. Separatism required a conceptual foundation of Bougainvillean identity; as distinct from a PNG or clan identity (Filer 1990). This politicization of identity led to changes in landownership through rhetorical appeals to "different and often contradictory principles of land tenure, or indeed any other aspect of social life … drawing upon a wide range of cultural norms and precedents" (Ballard 1997).

The combination of the indigenous communal land ownership system with colonization, resource extraction, incorporation into the PNG State and a separatist movement, has resulted in Bougainville having "polynormative, multilayered, and incomplete assertions of exclusionary property rights," that are often associated with post-colonial states (Fitzpatrick 2006). Despite this confusion, it is undeniable that underlying the evolving concepts of land there is an enduring connection to and concept of land as a critical part of society and identity in Bougainville.

Land also has many different facets and functions in Western societies. Three Western concepts of land in particular have had major impacts on peoples of the non-Western world. Firstly, Western societies have craved up the non-Western world into states. On a world map, all land and sea is bounded by black lines delineating the borders of states. Secondly, the

Western legal system is largely devoted to the enforcement of private property ownership, whether personal, corporate or state. This legal system is used to determine and protect ownership of land and land usage rights. Finally, economics, which is an inherently Western discipline, holds a very specific idea of land as a commodity. These three highly co-dependent Western concepts of land have evolved together and now constitute the dominant international paradigm for conceptualizing land and defining people's relationship to it. My focus in this chapter is on the differences between indigenous and economic concepts of land.

Economics understands land to be a very useful and powerful possession as it can be used as a factor of production in agriculture, forestry and mining. The ownership of factors of production, such as capital and land, are also the foundation of the economic class system in Marxist economics. When combined with the Western legal system, land can be exchanged, used as security on loans and as the basis of compensation claims. Enforcement of these legal transactions is largely dependent on the state. Furthermore, when combined with the state, the economic concept of land forms a basis for taxation and other forms of revenue collection, both formal and informal.

One critical economic concept of land is that of land as a commodity; something that can be bought and sold. Once land is sold, the original owner no longer has any economic rights to that land. Likewise, if the right to use or alter land in a certain way has been negotiated and paid for, the previous owner of the land has no right to complain or seek additional compensation. If this economic absolutism of land ownership is tempered in any way, then property rights are said to be "attenuated". This is a type of market failure that generates inefficiency, the nemesis of good economists the world over.

In order to be unattenuated, property rights must have the following characteristics: divisibility; transferability; duration; quality of title; and flexibility (Grafton, Squires and Fox 2000). In the context of property rights over land, which may be held directly or through a lease, the holder of those rights must be able to sell, lease or sub-lease part or all of their land in a fair land market. The rights must have a known and certain duration. In order to satisfy the requirements of quality of title and flexibility, the holder of property rights must be able to make decisions about the use of that land that are independent, without coercion or attempts to limit their control. Nearly all of the characteristics of unattenuated property rights are in conflict with Melanesian traditions. I will expand on the problems surrounding the transferability and quality of title in particular.

As rights to land use in Melanesia are held communally, with varied, overlapping and flexible rights to land ownership and usage amongst a community, the quality of title is diminished. There is no one person who has the right to make independent decisions about the use of land as there is no exclusive owner of that land. While the right to use a particular garden or hunting right may be transferred between individuals, the rights to use the land as a whole cannot be legitimately transferred by any individual. This has led to persistent calls by economists for land rights in Melanesia to be individualized, despite the obvious connection between communal land rights and the social structure of communities (Fingleton 2004).

In Melanesia, traditional rights to land "nearly always contained non-transferable ingredients which were either lost or retained by the transferer" when the land is sold (Sack 1973). Therefore, the quality of ownership experienced by a purchaser of land is not equal to that of the seller. This phenomenon is also evident in Western societies, in emotional attachments to places where people grew up, and in the frequent resistance of communities to residential developments. However, while non-transferability forms an essential part of Melanesian concepts of land, it is legally and economically irrelevant in modern Western societies (Sack 1973). Non-transferability is also the most critical of the ways in which economic property rights to land are attenuated in Melanesia.

The non-transferable elements of property rights in Melanesia are strongly linked with land as identity. While the right to hunt on land, to use it for plantation agriculture or to mine it can be sold, the purchaser does not acquire the same quality of ownership that would have been passed on to the traditional heirs of that land. If land is destroyed or alienated, the traditional owners lose that part of their identity that was bound up in the land with potentially damaging consequences for individuals and their communities. This aspect of Melanesian land rights is not only incompatible with economics, it is incomprehensible within the economic paradigm.

Land and the Bougainville Crisis

The Bougainville crisis began in 1988 with a sabotage campaign by indigenous Bougainvilleans against the Panguna mine, a copper mine that had been operating on Bougainville since 1969. The sabotage campaign escalated into more than a decade of violent conflict and a separatist struggle in which many people were killed and many more displaced from their homes. There has been a lively academic debate over the "real" cause of the crisis, which has most directly focused on the people of the Nasioi language group.

There are around 20,000 Nasioi people, many of whom were directly affected by the Panguna mine. Francis Ona, a Nasioi "big-man", became the leader of the separatist Bougainville Liberation Army (BLA) and self-proclaimed king of Bougainville. He claimed that he was defending Bougainville from "the threat of destruction by these foreign companies of mining" and that the PNG State wanted to "grab all of Bougainville for the sake (of the) economy of PNG" (Ona 1997).

The causes of the Bougainville crisis have been energetically debated. While recognizing the validity of the economic, environmental and political grievances of the Bougainvilleans, Colin Filer considers the critical factor to have been "a process of local social disintegration" (Filer 1990, Filer 1996). This social disintegration was bound up with the Melanesian big-man system, intergenerational conflict and the particular susceptibility of the Nasioi people to these problems. Wesley-Smith and Ogan presented a Marxist interpretation, citing class conflict fuelled by immigrant workers from other parts of PNG as a key cause of the crisis (Wesley-Smith and Ogan 1992). Kemelfield outlined a range of causes including: the role of land; immigration; perceptions of economic exploitation; and the repression tactics of the PNG police and military forces (Kemelfield 1992). This debate is unlikely to be resolved definitively as most of the explanations have some truth behind them.

Irrespective of the immediate trigger of the violence, there existed a range of grievances against the Panguna mine, the PNG State and between Bougainvilleans, all of which contributed to the conflict. Certainly one of the root causes of these grievances was land and forms of compensation for its destruction, use or pollution caused by mining activities. I propose that at a fundamental level these grievances were a result of the conflict between the concepts of land as identity and land as a commodity. Land was treated as a commodity by the mining company, as well as by those landowners who agreed to the mine and who accepted compensation for land use by the mining company. This resulted in a significant deterioration of indigenous social structure and contributing to the necessary conditions for the crisis to occur.

In 1973, only four years after the Panguna mine opened, Sack made the astute observation that, while indigenous systems of land rights remained, attitudes toward land were changing and that this, in turn, changed the way those rights were being used. He noted that Papua New Guineans were "aware of this change and usually explain it by saying that land was not as important to their forebears as it is to them," (Sack 1973). This was because land rights were acquiring a new meaning as an economic asset and commodity, as it could be used to earn cash income. Sack appreciated that, "being recognized as an economic asset reduces the importance of land in other respects" (Sack 1973). As holders of economic assets, owners of land rights had to make economic decisions about their use; and in many cases the rational, economic decision would be at odds with a decision made on the basis of social cohesion and the communal stability of land.

By agreeing to allow operation of the Panguna mine and by accepting compensation, individual Bougainvilleans made a decision to treat their land as an economic commodity. While traditional concepts of land and laws relating to ownership and usage remained, the engagement with these ideas and application of land usage rights was altered. Ownership and land use rights that were previously held communally and across generations were individualized, there was a single recognized decision-maker and land owner for the purposes of negotiation and receipt of compensation.

To claim that the Bougainvillean landowners affected by the Panguna mine did not understand what they were doing, were swindled out of their land and inadequately compensated is too simplistic. However, I would make two points. Firstly, the Panguna mine was, for a time, the largest open-cut mine in the world and it is unlikely that Bougainvilleans would have had an accurate idea of just how extensive the damage caused by the mine would be when they agreed to it. Secondly, the promise of dramatically increased standards of living through economic development was never fulfilled. While many Bougainvilleans did benefit from improved infrastructure and public services, they did not attain living standards equivalent to those that of a developed economy in return for the mine. The result of "the greater-than-expected negative impacts of the mine, and the lower-than-expected benefits" was resentment of the mine and also of the older generation of landowners that had made the original compensation deals with the mining company (May 2005). Subsequent generations of Bougainvilleans were denied the opportunity to make a decision for themselves about what was an acceptable trade off for the loss of their traditional ownership and usage rights to land.

The individualization of land usage rights in order to gain access to compensation from the Panguna mine was part of the process of commodification of land and damaged the traditional balance between communal and individual rights to land (Sack 1973). In addition, those non-transferable elements of land ownership, that could be inherited but not sold, were lost. For many, the land itself was unrecognizable; that part of their inheritance and history that had been bound up in the land was gone, and part of their identity lost. The resentment of the next generation of would-be landowners was reinforced by their lack of access to the compensation payments from the mining company (Filer 1990). When this resentment was acted out violently against the mine, the "bits of state" that existed in Bougainville, the police and security forces, aggravated the situation (Filer 1997).

As Ballard points out, traditional concepts of land do not "suggest that land in Melanesia cannot be commodified, but rather to make the obvious but not less important qualification that the social and cultural changes required to effect this transformation will have to be considerable," (Ballard 1997). This commodification of land was "the cost of engaging with the larger world of capital" and in the case of Bougainville, the cost became too high, the compensation inadequate and the constraints on violent conflict too weak (Ballard 1997).

Land and Economic Development

The economic orthodoxy considers provision of unattenuated property rights to be one of the central roles of the state and a necessary precondition for economic development. When considering the functions of the state, the World Bank listed provision of property rights as a minimal function along with "macroeconomic stability, control of infection diseases, safe water, roads, and the protection of the destitute," (World Bank 1997). These are considered to be the social, institutional and economic fundamentals in order to "avoid social disruption and ensure sustained development" (World Bank 1997). This displays the fundamental belief that without well-defined and enforced property rights over land, and other property, economic growth is not possible. In order for there to be unattenuated property rights over land, land must be transferable, which means that land must be a commodity.

Economic development is the goal of much economic policy and from an economic perspective, development is the primary purpose of the state (Fukuyama 2005). Consequently, many economists continue to promote the commodification of land. The idea of land as a commodity is deeply embedded in economics, and economics is embedded in Western society making it difficult for Western business people, bureaucrats, politicians, academics and policy makers to recognize or legitimatize any alternative concept of land.

Economics is seldom seen as being a cultural way of thinking, but rather it is advocated as being "scientific" and culturally neutral. This key assumption of cultural neutrality is challenged by indigenous concepts of land in places such as Bougainville. In Bougainville, treating land as a commodity was so culturally loaded that it eroded indigenous social institutions with devastating effects. The end result of this conflict between the ideas of land as a commodity and land as identity was social breakdown. Ironically, it is this type of "social disruption" that economics seeks to prevent through the enforcement of property rights. The developmental impact of the Bougainville crisis was negative with the destruction of property, disruption of the provision of services and widespread displacement of Bougainvillean peoples.

Let us consider the broader lessons from the experience of Bougainville for the pursuit of economic development in the broader Melanesian region. It may be noted that perhaps the most dangerous method of economics is to force an alien economic ideal into existing economic and social systems, forcing them to change to make them resemble that ideal. This type of thinking is often accompanied by the fallacy that there is only one path for development, the adoption of Westernized economic and legal systems. Typically, neoclassical economists argue that the attenuated property rights over land that occur under customary land tenure are preventing development and therefore must be changed (Huges 2004 and Gosarevski, Hughes and Windybank 2004). The insistence of such commentators that the only option for Melanesia is to develop and that this process requires land to be delineated, registered and divided into individual (as opposed to communal) ownership is a highly ideological position and one that is dismissed by many as too simplistic and culturally inappropriate.

However, there are many other economists who take more culturally appropriate approaches, using tools provided by institutional economics, which looks at existing social and economic structures and tries to make appropriate improvements. This approach compares favorably to those attempts to dismantle indigenous social and economic structures. Operating within existing indigenous institutions, changes in incentive structures are engineered to bring about desired changes in the outcomes that those institutions produce. This type of economics has gone some way in trying to reconcile communal land rights systems with economic property rights to land.

A range of economic problems have been identified in Melanesian land ownership: asymmetric information; time inconsistency of contracts; and incomplete contracts (Chand and Duncan 1997, Duncan and Duncan 1997, Lightfoot 2005, and McGavin 1993). The problems that these create are typically thought to be solvable using institutional economics. For example, an economic solution to the problem of attenuated property rights caused by insecure access to land would be to create contracts that are "more appropriate to the situation in these countries than contracts presently in use," or by adopting

> "other mechanisms that will lead to fewer disputes or to quicker resolution of disputes over contracts and therefore provide greater security to lessees and greater satisfaction to landowners and the government," (Duncan and Duncan 1997).

While these solutions are likely to have better results than the uncompromising stance of neoclassical economics, they are still in conflict with the fundamental "flexibility and fragility" of Melanesian societies and their ties to land (Filer 1990).

The creative contracting solutions from institutional economics may address issues of "duration" and "quality of title", but the problem of "transferability" remains. The layers of usage rights to land, covering both current and future generations, and non-transferable elements of ownership continue to lie beyond the reach of the most broad-minded and well-meaning of economists. What is of critical importance is that the concept of land as identity, which is held by Bougainvilleans, Melanesians and many other indigenous peoples, is outside of the paradigm of economics. The economic concept of land as a commodity is in direct conflict with a concept of land as identity as you cannot buy, sell or trade your identity. There is no solution to this conceptual conflict to be found within the discipline of economics.

Prospects for the Future

The conflict between the concepts of land held by Bougainvilleans, Melanesians and many other indigenous peoples, and the concept of land as a commodity that exists within economics, continues to generate social and economic disruption. The commodification of land weakens indigenous social structures and this deterioration hinders and sometimes reverses economic development. Historically, the principal economic solution for non-traditional usage of land has been monetary compensation. However, determining adequate monetary compensation for land may be impossible as the adequacy of the amount is not the real problem. The problem is the adequacy of money. The concept of land as identity is outside the economic paradigm, therefore solutions to this conflict must also be found outside the economic paradigm.

For Bougainvilleans, the memory of the conflict and distrust of the mining industry mean that it is unlikely that mining will be socially or politically viable in the near future. However, many are looking for ways to avoid the mistakes made in Bougainville and changing how land use rights are dealt with may be a vital first step. Solutions need to be found that minimize the disruption of those social institutions that prevent conflict, many of which are tied up with communal land use rights. Working with, rather than against, non-transferable indigenous customary land usage rights must be a part of this process.

The South Pacific Land Tenure Conflict Symposium held in 2002, stated in its declaration that "customary nature of land ownership and control in the Pacific ... does not prevent optimum use or development" (FAO/USP/RICS Foundation 2002). Furthermore, if land usage rights are viewed as primarily a social, rather than an economic phenomenon, an intellectual space can be created within which solutions can be sought (Weiner 2002). Pursuing changes to land tenure that are "gradualist and evolutionary" have the greatest chance of finding successful solutions to the problem of how to provide desirable economic development without generating significant and damaging conflicts (Holzknecht 2002). While these approaches hold great potential, they still face significant challenges in overcoming the entrenched orthodoxy that is rooted in economics.

In November 2005, a PNG Nation Land Summit was held with the objective of generating "strategic options to access land for development." In its main report, there is the familiar claim that:

> "(l)and cannot be used productively unless the property rights system which defines land rights is stable, secure and enforced. The objective of the new land policy, law, and administrative framework should be to define and enforce the land-user rights," (The Land Summit Coordinating Committee 2005).

This is a predictable, orthodox conclusion, and one that has had very limited success in the past. In PNG there are over forty Acts relating to land usages rights on non-customary land, these account for just three percent of PNG land (Armitage 2002), while the remaining 97 percent of land is held communally, outside the formal land laws of the PNG state.

Social disruption and conflicts will continue to occur in Melanesia and other indigenous societies where the introduction of the economic concept of land as a commodity undermines and delegitimizes the indigenous concept of land as identity. Extractive industries, such as mining and forestry, will continue to be a focus of this phenomenon. Compensation agreements made between extractive industries and indigenous landowners are often unstable. This instability borne from grievances against extractive industries, the state and those who are associated with them are likely to be expressed through physical violence.

Solutions to these conflicts may be achieved through addressing their root causes including the conflict between indigenous and economic concepts of land. It is important to begin by understanding the way in which the commodification of land undermines the indigenous concept of land as identity. This directly undermines the social fabric of indigenous communities. Likewise, the impact of indigenous concepts of land of economic property rights, hindering the potential for beneficial economic development, should be taken into consideration. Reconciling these concepts is a difficult task, but it is of critical importance for Melanesians and other indigenous communities worldwide.

Works Cited

Armitage, Lynne. 2002. *Land Tenure in Papua New Guinea: Custom and Commerce at the Interface A Case Study of the Ahi People's Land, Morobe Province, PNG.* accessed at: www.usp.ac.fj/landmgmt/pdf/webpapers/paper61armitage.pdf (Accessed on 11 November 2006).

Ballard, Chris. 1997. "It's the land, stupid! The moral economy of resource ownership in Papua New Guinea," in Peter Lamour (ed), *The Governance of Common Property in the Pacific Region*, pp 47-66. Canberra: National Center for Development Studies and Resource Management in Asia-Pacific, Research School of Pacific and Asian Studies, The Australian National University.

Boydell, Spike. 2001. *Land Tenure and Land Conflict in the South Pacific: Consultancy Report for the Food and Agriculture Organisation (FAO) of the United Nations.* Suva: USP Solutions, University of the South Pacific.

Chand, Satish and Ron Duncan. 1997. "Resolving property issues as a precondition for growth: access to land in the Pacific islands," in Peter Lamour (ed), *The Governance of Common Property in the Pacific Region,* pp 33-46. Canberra: National Center for Development Studies and Resource Management in Asia-Pacific, Research School of Pacific and Asian Studies, The Australian National University.

Dove, J., T. Miriung, and M. Togolo. 1974. "Mining bitterness," in Peter G. Sack (ed), *Problem of Choice: Land in Papua New Guinea's Future*, pp 181-189. Canberra and Port Moresby: Australian National University Press and Robert Brown and Associates.

Duncan, Ron and Rod Duncan. 1997. "Improving security of access to customary-owned land in Melanesia: mining in Papua New Guinea," in Peter Lamour (ed), *The Governance of Common Property in the Pacific Region*, pp 73-88. Canberra: National Center for Development Studies and Resource Management in Asia-Pacific, Research School of Pacific and Asian Studies, The Australian National University.

FAO/USP/RICS Foundation South Pacific Land Tenure Conflict Symposium. 2002. *Declaration* accessed at: www.usp.ac.fj/landmgmt/pdf/spltcdeclarationresolutions.pdf (accessed on 11 November 2006).

Filer, Colin. 1990. "The Bougainville Rebellion, the Mining Industry and the Process of Social Disintegration in Papua New Guinea," in R. J. May and Matthew Spriggs (eds), *The Bougainville Crisis*, pp 73-112. Bathurst: Crawford House Press, Bathurst.

Filer, Colin. 1996. "Compensation, Rent and Power in Papua New Guinea," in S. Toft (ed), *Compensation for Resource Development in Papua New Guinea*, pp 156-189. Canberra: National Centre for Development Studies, Australian National University.

Filer, Colin. 1997. "The Melanesian way of menacing the mining industry," in Ben Burt and Christian Clerk (eds), *Environment and Development in the Pacific Islands*, pp 91-122. Canberra: National Center for Development Studies, Australian National University.

Fingelton, Jim (ed). 2005. *Privatizing Land in the Pacific: A Defense of Customary Tenures*, Discussion Paper No. 80, June 2005. Canberra: The Australia Institute.

Fingleton, Jim. 2004. "Is Papua New Guinea viable *without* customary groups?" *Pacific Economic Bulletin*, Vol. 19, No. 2, pp 96-103. Canberra: Asia Pacific Press, Australian National University.

Fukuyama, Francis. 2005. "'Stateness' First," *Journal of Democracy,* Vol 16, No. 1, January 2005, pp 84-88. Washington: Johns Hopkins University Press.

Grafton, R, D. Squires and K. Fox. 2000. "Private Property and Economic Efficiency: A Study of Common-pool Resources," *Journal of Law and Economics*, Vol. XLIII, October 2000, pp 679-714. Chicago: University of Chicago Press.

Gosarevski, Steven, Helen Hughes, and Susan Windybank. 2004. "Is Papua New Guinea viable *with* customary land ownership?" *Pacific Economic Bulletin*, Vol. 19, No. 3, 2004, pp 133-136. Canberra: Asia Pacific Press, Australian National University.

Holzknect, Hartmut. 2002. *Regional Representatives Report: Papua New Guinea,* accessed at :

www.usp.ac.fj/landmgmt/pdf/webpapers/pngpaper.pdf (Accessed on 11 November 2006).

Hughes, Helen. 2004. "The Pacific is Viable!" *Issue Analysis*, No. 53, December 2004. The Center for Independent Studies, accessed at www.cis.org.au on 10 May 2005.

Kemelfield, Graeme. 1992. "Reflections on the Bougainville conflict: underlying causes and conditions for a resolution," in Matthew Spriggs and Donald Denoon (eds), *The Bougainville Crisis: 1991 Update*, pp 152-160. Bathurst: Crawford House Press.

The Land Summit Coordinating Committee. 2005. *The National Land Summit: Report for the Minister for Lands and Physical Planning: Part 2: Main Report* accessed at : www.nri.org.pg/pages/landsummit_nldt_files/National%20Land%20Summit%20Report% 20Part%202.pdf (Accessed on 11 November 2006).

Lightfoot, Chris. 2005. "Does customary land ownership make economic sense?" *Privatizing Land in the Pacific: A Defense of Customary Tenures*, Discussion Paper No. 80, June 2005, pp 22-27. Canberra: The Australia Institute.

May, R. J. 2005. "Conflict Resolution: Lessons from Bougainville" Christchurch conference paper. Unpublished.

McGavin, P.A. 1993. *Economic Security in Melanesia: Key Issues for Managing Contract Stability and Mineral Resources Development in Papua New Guinea, Solomon Islands, and Vanuatu.* Honolulu: Pacific Islands Development Program, Research Report Series No.16, East-West Center.

Ona, Francis. 1997. Transcript of "Interview with Francis Ona," *World in Focus*, Broadcast March 1997, interviewed by Coles-Janess, Wayne.Australian Broadcasting Corporation, accessed at: www.abc.net.au/foreign.stories.s400627.htm (Accessed on 10 May 2005).

Reagan, Anthony J. 2002. "The Bougainville political settlement and the prospects for sustainable peace," *Pacific Economic Bulletin*, pp 114-129, Volume 17, Number 1, May 2002. Canberra: Asia Pacific Press, Australian National University.

Sack, Pater G. 1973. *Land Between Two Laws: Early European Land Acquisitions in New* Guinea. Canberra: Australian University Press.

Saovana-Spriggs, Ruth. 2003. "Bougainville women's role in conflict resolution in the bougainville peace process," in Sinclair Dinnen, Anita Jowitt and Tess Newton-Cain (eds), *A Kind of Mending: Restorative*

Justice in the Pacific Islands. Canberra: Pandanus Press, Australian National University.

Weiner, James. 2002. *Adverse Possession: Some observations on the relation between land and land-based knowledge in Papua New Guinea.*accessed at : www.usp.ac.fj/landmgmt/pdf/webpapers/paperx1weiner.pdf (Accessed on 11 November 2006).

Wesley-Smith, Terence and Ogan, Eugene. 1992. "Copper, Class and Crisis: Changing Relations of Production in Bougainville," *The Contemporary Pacific*, pp 245-267, Volume 4, Number 2, Fall 1992. Honolulu: University of Hawai'i Press.

The World Bank. 1997. *World Development Report 1997: The State in a Changing World.* New York: Oxford University Press.

CHAPTER SIX

CULTURAL CONCEPTIONS OF DISC PIRACY IN CHINA: STRUCTURAL CONSTRAINTS AND LOCAL LEVEL POLICY IMPLEMENTATION

MATT WEST

Introduction

One of the defining features of our time has been the vast growth of the "knowledge economy." The term itself has become ubiquitous in the framing of all sorts of questions about positioning and maintaining the niche of a city, province, or country within a global economy (for China, see for instance Huang 2006, Ma 2006). While much of this talk addresses education or knowledge in general, the very existence of the knowledge economy itself is founded on the idea of ownership of intellectual property or "IP." Through IP rights, an author or inventor is given a monopoly for a limited time over profits from her work in exchange for completely revealing it to the public. While IP is commonly said to encompass patents, copyrights, and trademarks, it has also been used to include indigenous rights, cultural property rights, and trade secrets among others. This chapter will focus primarily on copyright.[1]

Coming at the issue of IP and the knowledge economy from a broadly social scientific perspective, IP's beginning and expansion has effectively been the *creation* of new categories of ownership. In the past we could not

---

[1] A version of this chapter was originally presented at the 5th East-West Center International Graduate Student Conference, Honolulu, Hawai'i, February 2006. I would like to thank the participants in my panel as well as the other presenters for their suggestions both during and after the panel. The research for this contribution was conducted with funding from the Chinese University of Hong Kong as partial fulfillment of the requirements of the Department of Anthropology's M.Phil. program.

own things like songs, stories, minority dances, seed germplasm, or modified DNA. It was not that we did not have them. We just could not individually own them like we could tangible property. Now, not only can these be owned, but they also can be bought, sold, licensed, and stolen. This creation, rather than any sort of innate right to ownership, has then been the origin of "piracy."

In order to address the cultural conceptions of intellectual property essential to this ongoing process of creation, I plan to make use of observational and interview data I collected while conducting fieldwork in Xi'an, China in the summer of 2005. After outlining some recent work on IP, the chapter will introduce stories from Chenggong, its owners, and customers to highlight how morality and legality intersect with piracy when it is seen primarily as a retail business. I will also address some issues related to the enforcement of IP laws and their consequences at the local level. The chapter will conclude with some suggestions and considerations I take to be essential for constructing viable IP policy.

Intellectual Property and China

In 2003, the Motion Picture Association of America estimated their losses of "potential revenue" to be in the neighborhood of 178 million US dollars (2004). According to the Recording Industry Association of America (RIAA): "piracy in China for all categories of copyrighted materials exceeds 90 percent [of all products sold, and 95 percent of the music sector]" (Rosen 2003). These figures are despite the fact that, over the same period, the Chinese government seized 68 million pirated discs in raids along with several illicit production lines (National Copyright Administration of the PRC 2004). It then should not be a surprise that China is the target of bilateral and multilateral attempts to crackdown on piracy.

It may, however, be a surprise to know that this pressure is not recent. The Qing dynasty was the first to be forced to adopt foreign IP protection laws in the beginning of the 20th century. According to Alford (1995), where Imperial China *did have* limitations on copying and sharing knowledge, these were meant exclusively to maintain imperial power through censorship, not to protect authors rights or promote innovation. Neither these first treaties, nor the more formal laws enacted later by the Qing, Nationalist, and Communist governments under similar pressure, arose from domestic traditions, social norms, or concerns raised by Chinese businesses, authors, or inventors. The case of China then, a place where these non-indigenous concepts have not yet been completely constructed, or at least have not yet become fully entrenched, provides valuable support and information on the process of constructing such laws.

It is important to recognize that, not only in China, but also worldwide, IP is a politically constructed policy and *not* a natural right. We have not always been able to own intangible property and there is nothing about it that makes it "natural" to do so. Political economists and sociologists explain that the establishment and expansion of IP both nationally and internationally has been based on the power and particular interests of specific actors including states like Britain and the United States as well as the loose coalition of businesses that lobbied for the TRIPs agreement (see May 1998, Mathews 2002).

Lawrence Lessig (2004) takes this political argument a step further to describe the historical progression many such actors took from piracy to copyright advocacy. States, businesses, and individuals tend to begin their careers as pirates. As they themselves accumulate a store of "intellectual capital" in the form of IP, their position changes. The United States, copying British writers, and Hollywood, evading patents on the film projector, for instance, were both notorious pirates in their early histories (*ibid.*: 19). Lessig continues to explain that IP can actually slow down or prevent innovation, an observation receiving increasing support from economists as well (see Granstrand 1999: 41, Lerner 2002). As an example, Lessig explains how RCA, by buying up the patents for FM radio, was able to prevent its release for 20 years. Through their use of patents, RCA protected their own investment in an extensive AM radio network, while at the same time the new technology, promising a much clearer signal, was kept from advancing (Lessig 2004: 67).

Filling in this picture of political construction, Siva Vaidhynathan (2001) explains how the romantic view of the author helped to frame the political debate in the United States. Figures like Webster, Twain, and Disney each have played significant roles in lobbying congress to "respect authors' rights" and strengthen IP. As a tribute to the strength of their advocacy for IP as an "author's right," in at least one federal court ruling a judge supported his position over a parent's right to frozen human embryos by talking of the natural right an author has to the work to which he gave "birth" (Strathern 1999). At the same time, however, the way copyright works in practice is that the majority of authors must sell out their rights to companies to get their work published at all. The owners of copyrights thus tend to be publishers and production companies rather than the artists or authors themselves. Yet, as a result of this ideological push, the duration of copyright terms has been extended from 14 years in 1790 (in which one had to register to gain protection at all) to the author's life plus 70 years in 1998 (with no need to register or renew protection) in the United States. IP then is not merely the creation of new categories of ownership, but also specifically is the continued expansion of those categories in ways that benefit particular interest groups.

Chenggong Music and Movies

Returning to the case of China, the majority of my participant observation data was collected in a retail music and movies shop called Chenggong Music and Movies.[2] Mr. and Mrs. Wang opened Chenggong Music and Movies almost a decade ago in the same place they are now as one of the area's first such stores. Continuous renovations have been especially important since a chain shop moved in a block or two away. They explained to me that competition in the disc business in Xi'an is fierce. By changing their appearance every once in a while they can cultivate a modern look that allows them a slightly higher price and thus some profit to live off of.

The store is opened in the mornings by Mr. Wang and Xiao Zhang, a teenager who migrated to the city from the countryside. Mr. Wang takes all of the cash from Chenggong at nights, but, like the other shops on the street, one employee sleeps inside to keep an eye on the merchandise. Together, Xiao Zhang and Mr. Wang move various display racks, pricing posters, and chairs out of their storage places and onto the sidewalk just in front of the shop. They fold up the boy's bed and store it in a back room owned by the same state-owned company who rents them their space. By 7 am, the store is open for business and I sit with Mr. Wang on the sidewalk in the shade of a tree talking and waiting.

Throughout the day a variety of customers stop into Chenggong. During the lagtime between customers, I spoke with them about intangible property, current events from the daily newspapers, and the lottery. Nearly everyday, at least two or three of Mr. Wang's friends would stop by to chat and smoke a cigarette. While the most frequent of these was the manager of the company he rents space from, others included the lottery saleswoman down the street, people who have or used to have shops nearby, a lawyer, and someone in the local police bureau.

Chenggong is, in many ways, a typical disc store.[3] Unlike its chain

---

[2] Keeping with anthropological tradition and in respect to my informants' privacy, all of the names in this chapter are pseudonyms.

[3] In Xi'an, there are several kinds of disc sellers with street front stores being only one. In addition to these Chenggong-types of stores, there are also wandering vendors and clustering vendors. Wandering vendors walk the streets in particular

competitor, it does not have air conditioning, glass windows, or tiled floors. Instead, much like the majority of smaller shops, it has concrete floors, is open air, and short on decorations. The store is located in Xi'an's central walled district, off the main roads but close enough to have steady foot traffic passing by. The store sells cassette tapes, CDs, VCDs, and DVDs. Around 80 percent of the music is Chinese language with the rest being an odd mixture of currently popular Western titles and perennial Chinese favorites like Michael Jackson, the Backstreet Boys, and Richard Marx. The movie selections are predominately from Hollywood, but may have German, French, or Russian titles and are increasingly mixed in with Japanese, Korean, and Chinese productions. Importantly, Wang Ge sells mainly unlicensed or, pirated discs, but also has a few poorly selling licensed titles that accumulate dust in a corner.

Consuming Pirated Discs

While it is easy to spot bad quality pirated discs, the differences between the good quality ones and the licensed ones are extremely small. My informants could come up with a whole list of things to look at including the packaging, the colors, picture quality, English mistakes, the quality of the recording, and even the number of copyright warnings that appear before the main feature. Yet, in the end, they admitted that they largely had no idea which was which. In fact, Wang Ge bought his pirated discs from the same wholesalers as stores several of my informants claimed had to sell licensed discs (such as the nearby chain shop). For most then, the decision on what and where to buy came down to a balance of price and quality. Asking a shopkeeper if their discs were licensed or pirated was more about learning if the shopkeeper would guarantee the quality. The response, "of course it's licensed, if there's a problem, just bring it back" suited most customers just fine.

People invariably told me that they bought only pirated discs and did so without any guilty feelings. The manager of the company Chenggong rents space from explained that,

---

areas selling discs out of boxes, blankets, or their coats. While this type of seller is quite common in Beijing and Shenzhen (and in New York for that matter), it is less common in Xi'an. Clustering vendors also sell from boxes, but at relatively fixed locations that they share with other disc vendors. They tend to set up semi-permanent stalls in the basements or upper floors of electronics markets and stay there for months at a time. Sharing space with other disc vendors helps both to attract customers and to provide cooperation in the case of a police raid.

> "Ninety-nine in 100 people will buy the cheaper one and the others will look at that one person and laugh, not understanding. Even the Governor and the Mayor (*shengzhang* and *shizhang*) buy pirated discs. They buy it because it's cheaper, of course, they get someone else to go and do the buying for them, but they don't buy the 100 yuan one, they buy the one for 6."

My informants thought it was ridiculous to expect a person with their income to spend the price of a licensed disc just to watch a single movie. They were unwilling to pay more because they would only watch it once or twice and then set it aside. Rich people might be able to afford that, but poorer people also deserve to be able to see and share in the content of the disc. Through such cheap discs, they could keep up with the latest trends and singers. Pirated movies and music was seen as an accessible piece of modernity that they could consume on par with rich people in developed countries and in cities along China's coast. The only time my informants said they made an effort to buy licensed discs was as gifts for people of the same or higher social position. In this case, however, rather than the intangible property on the disc, the more important factor was the higher price and quality of the gift which could better portray the value of their friendship.

Morality and Illegality

While all of my informants knew that pirated discs were illegal, they did not think buying or selling them amounted to stealing as one 20 year old female informant said:

> "You pay for it. You give the person money and they give you the disc. How could this be stealing? Pirated discs are cheap so poor people buy them. It is not stealing."

The only time stealing occurred was the first time that someone made a copy, at the manufacturing stage. At this stage, the disc was copied without any exchange of money. This could be considered stealing, but the remaining stages were simply people making a living like anyone else. To consumers, piracy is just a business.

When I asked if someone would look down on them for buying a pirated disc like others might for buying knock-off clothes, my informants, young and old, said "of course not." As everyone buys it, there is no reason for anyone to be looked down on. While piracy is clearly illegal, it is not seen as immoral. I was told on many occasions that morality should be seen not as absolute, but as relative. Disc piracy provides access to something that poorer people would have no access to otherwise. It provides much needed money and start up capital that stays in the area and helps local development. As they saw it, pirated discs do no harm to people. They are not at all like fake medicines or fake foods that could make someone seriously ill.

Most people stressed that the ambiguous position it occupies is less due to the products sold and more due to how the business is run. Retail business in general is seen as a morally ambiguous entity. Shopkeepers are constantly accused of cheating, especially of cheating outsiders, both by charging too high a price or passing off low quality goods as high. As a male informant explained,

> "Every kind of business definitely has cheating in it. China has a saying to describe this, *wushang bujian*.[4] I can explain it like this: Business people are driven by economic benefits. My goal is only to make money. Therefore I may use shadowy methods to make that money, including cheating. I produce some things using fake raw materials, but from the outside they look like the real one. In business, for instance, even when we're negotiating on a contract there is also deception. Absolutely there can be. There isn't one industry that could say that there isn't deception."

This ambivalence is definitely not a result of the Chinese being unaccustomed to market exchange, as both urban and rural people in China have been involved in markets for centuries (Cohen 2005: 4). Rather, it builds on both selectively chosen "traditional" Chinese cultural ideas and more recent political and historical trends. Traditionally, merchants were part of the lowest class rank under scholar-officials, farmers, and craftsmen in dynastic China due to their outsider status as well as reputations for cheating. In addition to the saying quoted above, which is common in Taiwan as well, numerous other sayings also supported the fact that such historic attitudes were still relevant and being drawn upon in the present.

This ambivalence has also partially been a result of suspicions of private businesses that emerged at the beginning of China's reform period. As Bruun (1993) points out, in the early reform period, businesses were opened by people of lower social status and due to raw material shortages, nearly all businesses had to skirt illegality just to do business at all. Where earlier there was only one route to success, through the party/work unit, there now emerged a group of richer people who, despite their riches, had

---

[4] Literally, this means "no business does not deceive."

not outgrown their low social standing. As a result of this double ladder of wealth and prestige, some attempted to trade success on one ladder for entry onto the other. Business people began to try to enter the government (often through volunteer work) and government workers began to dabble in business (Bruun 1993). My informants emphasized how many government officials used their connections to "get rich first." The large profits some businesses made were, and are still, seen as resulting less from hard work, and more from cheating or connections in the government.

Despite such a morally ambiguous position, I was frequently reminded that everyone must have a way to earn their own rice. My informants said it should not make any difference to them (or to me) how someone else makes theirs. While they saw retail business as an ambivalent entity, many younger informants wanted to go into private business and many of my older friends were already engaged in it. People simply accepted that the clear goal of business is to make a profit, not to serve its customers. As with the quotation above, my informants agreed that the boss' goal drove their actions and that they therefore would use any and all means to be certain to achieve that goal, just as customers would try to do the same to get a lower price. While several informants told me they would never shop at a family member's shop out of fear that they would be forced to buy something similar to what they wanted at a higher price (rather than exactly what they wanted at a bargained price), customers also commonly tried to pull on commonalties like ethnicity, *laojia* (or ancestral home), or schooling ties to bargain prices down.

Retail business is thus neither absolutely moral nor absolutely immoral, and it is then in this context that we can see selling unlicensed discs as a relatively moral business. Piracy is not seen as stealing. It is a business and makes a profit, but that profit is to support someone's family and, as a trade, it is not any worse than many others.

Structures of Enforcement

In spite of these attitudes toward piracy on the part of retail businesses and consumers, the practice remains illegal in China. Furthermore, the Chinese government is under continued pressure from foreign interest groups as well as increasing pressure from domestic interests to show results for its crackdowns. Yet these crackdowns do not seem to produce the results that the music and movie industries are looking for. Here, I will deal with three primary structural issues that scholars (see Bakken 2005, Dutton 2005, and Mertha 2005) have pointed to within the Chinese enforcement community and their repercussions on the local level of policy implementation, which include campaign style police actions, the moral role of the police, and the institutional structure of copyright enforcement.

First, policing in China during the reform period has continued the practice common in the Maoist period of campaign style police actions. These *yanda,* or "strike hard," campaigns are meant to focus police and mass resources over a short period of time on a particular problem. By highlighting one illegal activity at a time they are meant to have a large impact on that specific arena of crime both in the short-term by making many arrests and successful prosecutions and in the long-term by serving as a drastic warning to those who were not caught to give up the practice. Campaigns are characterized by large pressure on police to make many arrests, perform quick trials, and severely punish the guilty as examples. Instead, however, Tanner (2005: 179) finds that such "special struggles" become routine. In Harbin for instance, 340 days in 1988 were designated as part of different campaign actions. Each day the police were meant to be fighting a different "key element" in crime. This focus actually diverts attention from the regular daily roles of the police in favor of concentrated action. Criminals tend to know when such campaigns are coming (they are often seasonal, centering on particular holidays or other announcements) and structure their activity accordingly (*ibid.*: 179). Thus only relatively marginal offenders with fewer connections and backing, like migrants (who are also often the most frequent crime victims), tend to be targeted and caught (Bakken 2005: 75).

To give an example of the importance of connections in crackdowns on disc piracy, all of the DVDs mysteriously disappeared from Chenggong for about a week during August. Although the business was open as usual, all of the DVDs had been removed and their places were taken up with extra copies of VCDs and CDs that were already displayed elsewhere. One of the workers informed me simply that the government had told them to get rid of them and, with a bit of sarcasm, added that "we always listen to the police." Mr. Wang later explained that it was only a temporary thing and that, before too long they would be able to sell them again. All of the normal DVDs had been "sold" (though I guess this meant taken back to the distributor) and the boxed sets were stashed in a drawer. When customers came in asking for DVDs, they simply said they did not have any. Occasionally, Mr. Wang would also add that they should check back in a few days.

During the period the discs were gone, a lawyer stopped by to talk with Mr. Wang. Besides talking with me about the uselessness of lawyers in

China, however, Mr. Wang was not willing to talk any more about the incident. I am thus left uncertain if this conversation implied that Chenggong had been fined or had been in danger of being fined, but I suspect that a warning of a raid which then did not occur was involved. Interestingly, if there was a raid or possible fine, it seemed only to concern DVDs rather than any of the other merchandise. Furthermore, while other shops in the general area also had gotten rid of their DVDs, besides this removal, all else ran like normal and by the next week the DVDs too were back.[5] I was told on several occasions when talking to other friends about this instance that the type of connections Mr. Wang seemed to have were similar to those needed by most other stores as well. Campaigns could come up on anything, ranging from not having proper licenses (which Chenggong actually did have) to inspections for fake goods to raids on real goods sold outside their licensed distribution range.

The second aspect of policing is their historical role relating to morality. While police everywhere, like other members of society, are influenced by local morals and norms, police in communist China were seen as needing to "take care of the moral order rather than the impersonal black letter law" (Dutton 2005: 83). They were the power that then helped define and enforce the morality of the dictatorship of the proletariat. Officially through 1997, though perhaps living on in practice, police were instructed to apply the law "analogously." This means, for example, that although there was no law making adultery illegal, it was still seen as immoral and was still prosecuted. Police simply prosecuted adultery under the law against rape. Adulterers could thus be sentenced analagously according to the rape guidelines (Bakken 2005: 2). With this type of moral mandate, local police had significant discretion to enforce moral and social norms much as local officials were given such power in dynastic times (Alford 1995: 24). In a sense, as it applies to pirated discs, this discretion could work in reverse. While piracy is proscribed by law, it is not seen as immoral and thus police might not prosecute it (especially if pressed through funding by local officials). As an action that is not perceived as immoral, police might choose either only to prosecute piracy cases during a campaign or only when the business also breaks more morally relevant laws like those against pornography.

---

[5] The owners of several daoban music and movie stores that Mertha (2005: 144) describes running into during his research also explained that during campaigns they would temporarily hide their illegal discs. After the campaign finished, the illegal discs would come back out and the status quo returns. One owner even told him directly to come back next week (when the campaign would finish and he could again sell daoban discs).

A third structural aspect to piracy concerns the institutional arrangement of copyright enforcement agencies within the Chinese bureacracy. The overriding concern and limiting aspects of copyright enforcement agencies are their small budgets, their relatively weak positions within their parent bureau (the Press and Publications Bureau, PPB), and the fact that copyright enforcement is low on its parent bureau's list of goals. Although members may not like the idea of pirate publishers remaining unregulated, they also recognize that, in the face of resource scarcity, they have no way to completely enforce the law. Thus they tend to "pursue those pirated products that provide a clear threat to social stability and the political status quo" (Mertha 2005: 19). As with the police, this would lead them to concentrate on pornography or other types of censorship rather than regular unlicensed discs, a concentration which, not coincidentally, also fit better with the larger bureau's overall goal.

The PPB is split organizationally into five subsections including books, periodicals, anti-pornography and anti-illegal publishing, distribution, and copyright. While several of these subsections and the PPB itself extend from the national level all the way down to local levels, the copyright subsection has staff members only down to the provincial level. They must therefore depend on other subsections' people (mainly the "cultural market" management group dealing with pornography and illegal publishing) to coordinate enforcement actions (Mertha 2005: 149). These subsections, however, have their own goals and must use their own limited resources to attain *those* goals first. Pornography not only becomes a morally convenient target for police, but also an organizationally easier target to crack down on. According to a 1999 book by the Economic Intelligence Unit (Hong Kong),

> "the PPB, [the National Copyright Administration's (NCA) parent body,] is concerned mainly with censorship and has no interest in promoting the rights of authors or creating a free market in publishing. The [NCA's] lack of funding is at least partially because of a conscious decision by the PPB to ignore copyright issues" (Economist Intelligence Unit 1999: 51 quoted in Mertha 2005: 140).

Social Consequences of Enforcement

As the above discussion of morality and enforcement might suggest, the relationship between crackdowns on pornography and those on pirated discs has had interesting effects at the local level. The Chinese government as well as the music and movie industries in the United States both actively associate pirated discs with pornography. In the United

States, this association has the support of religious conservatives as well as a valuable moral basis for anti-piracy campaigns, especially those against file-sharing. The industry could claim that, in addition to transferring knowledge and MP3s, Napster and other downloading services were being used to expose children to pornographic images (Hansell 2003). For China, this combination meant that they could crackdown on pornography, a target of censorship since at least the Song Dynasty in 1009 (Alford 1995: 21), under the cover of a crackdown on pirated discs without criticism from activists advocating freedom of speech.

One such combination of campaigns occurred and was widely reported in the summer of 2006, a year after my fieldwork in Xi'an ended. This nationwide campaign against pirated discs was meant to last 100 days and was touted in the People's Daily's English newspaper as one focusing on "pirated audio-video products and computer software" (People's Daily 2006). The article goes on to describe the campaign's success saying that police and copyright officials had seized over eight billion illegal products, raided more than 89 thousand shops and vendors, punished nine thousand of them, and closed down over three thousand stores over the course of the first month of the campaign. Furthermore, the same article states that "more than 60 percent of shops nationwide registered in the audio-video trade had handed in pirated discs they were storing." A Chinese language update on the same campaign, while also mentioning arrests in relation to pirated discs, describes the arrest of people involved in pornography as one of the important victories of the campaign (Renmin Ri Bao 2006). The constellation of structural influences and priorities described in prior sections has meant that this campaign, as with most others, focuses both on pornography and pirated discs.

At a local level this dual emphasis on pornography and piracy has indeed meant that pirated discs have been somewhat successfully linked to pornography. However, this has not made all pirated discs seem "yellow" or dirty. It has not given piracy the lower moral position of pornography. Instead, pornography is seen by some, especially in more rural areas, as the only kind of "pirated" discs. Non-pornographic discs must just be of varying qualities of licensed discs. In short, this has made non-pornographic pirated discs more, rather than less moral. In this way, the meaning of the Chinese terms for pirated or licensed discs have less and less to do with IP and more to do with their local contexts. While pornographic materials, many of which come in disc form, were sold fairly openly in stores when I lived in Xi'an in 2001, they are now largely relegated to the clustering vendors category of sellers and are unavailable at most streetfront shops. Not selling pornography allows Chenggong and other shops to appear more legitimate and more "licensed" to consumers (and police). This also helps to shelter them from a large portion of raids.

In the pirated disc market, clustering vendors are often targeted as they have more discs to seize for each raid. They also have pornographic selections and may not have good enough connections in the relevant departments to protect themselves. For the police, such an emphasis boosts their statistics and makes them appear more successful: a raid on a single location produces a larger number of arrests and many more discs. Also importantly, they do not have to compromise their own connections or raid what are seen as more legitimate stores. It is not inconceivable that, in order to produce such high numbers in the 2006 campaign, police and copyright agencies targeted clustering vendors for raids while also calling in on their own connections to promote the "voluntary" surrender of discs.

Conclusion

By way of conclusion, I wish to highlight a few main points. If you are trying to distinguish between licensed and pirated discs, the market for music and movies in Xi'an is largely characterized by confusion. There is no good way to tell the difference. Even large chain stores selling at higher prices may only be selling good quality pirated products at higher profit margins. Licensed and unlicensed, in this context then do not translate into real and fake. As with the pornography example above, the perceived difference between "licensed" and "pirated" discs may have little to do with intellectual property. Instead, the two are seen as two poles along a scale of quality and price. As a result, consumers focus on buying where the price and relative quality fits their own financial situation. Though poorer consumers will tell you that richer ones buy licensed, in fact, the richer consumers I spoke to merely bought more and better quality pirated discs. Thus they focus on the physical disc and how the store looks, not on the intangible property. As for enforcement, police and the PPB, in addition to structural issues, are tasked with stopping an illegal activity which is largely seen as a relatively moral business. More stores have moved away from pornography and, in doing so, these stores appear to consumers (and perhaps to the police) as more legitimate no matter what type of disc content they sell.

These themes bring up several important policy-oriented questions. Firstly, while many economic or political economy studies successfully focus on the growth, impact, and networks of piracy in a globalized world, they often then miss the local contexts. Piracy is framed as a network, affiliated with organized crime and even linked to terrorism. While all of this may have an element of truth to it, its characterization of piracy as a single monolithic evil entity is patently misleading as policy is concerned. Because policy must always, in the end, be implemented at local levels, the fact that there are multiple types of disc stores in Xi'an competing fiercely with one another is important. It is also essential to understand that none of these are easily identified as shops selling licensed discs, at least not in the way that IP defines the word licensed. In the eyes of consumers, shop owners, and the police, certain categories of these stores are more or less legitimate, more or less moral. At this level it is viewed as a relatively moral business that does little harm, not as terrorism or organized crime.

The association of the Chinese terms for licensed and pirated discs with contextual issues rather than with the presence or absence of IP is also telling. Clearly, despite 100 years of history with IP laws on the books in China, a concept of ownership of intangible ideas similar to the West has not yet been constructed. The United States, China, and other governments should be willing to (re)fit IP law closer to local practice. This would then make the laws enforceable both through legal measures as well as through social norms of morality. As Lessig suggests, governments should recognize that advocacy for IP may only come as the people, business, or country builds up its own (competing) store of intellectual capital.

As IP does not always enhance innovation, and sometimes hinders it (especially for developing countries) we should actively explore other options and systems that might have broader benefits. Finally, my informants stressed that the United States should not always be concerned with money. It should instead see the benefits of piracy, especially in cases of unequal access due to poverty and/or censorship, in providing a window for many into modernity and other cultures. While piracy is often portrayed in the media as linked to organized crime and corruption of some sort, it is not always the case. In many cases, when looked at from a local level, it is simply seen as another type of retail business. It is their way of spreading knowledge and earning rice for their family.

Works Cited

Alford, William P. 1995. *To Steal a Book is an Elegant Offense: Intellectual Property Law in Chinese Civilization.* Stanford: Stanford University Press.

Bakken, Børge (ed.). 2005. *Crime, Punishment, and Policing in China.* Lanham, MD: Rowman and Littlefield Publishers.

Bruun, Ole. 1993. *Business and Bureaucracy in a Chinese City: An Ethnography of Private Business Households in Contemporary China.* Berkeley, California: Institute of East Asian Studies, University of California.

"China closes 3,000 shops in crackdown on pirated CDs, DVDs." 2006. *People's Daily Online,* 17 August, at http://english.peopledaily.com.cn/200608/17/eng20060817_293979.html (accessed 5 February 2007).

Cohen, Myron. 2005. *Kinship, Contract, Community, and State: Anthropological Perspectives on China.* Stanford: Stanford University Press.

Dutton, Michael. 2005. "Toward a Government of the Contract: Policing in the Era of Reform," in Børge Bakken (ed.), *Crime, Punishment, and Policing in China*, pp. 189-233. Lanham, MD: Rowman and Littlefield Publishers.

Economist Intelligence Unit. 1999. *China Hand: The Complete Guide to Doing Business in China.* Hong Kong: Economist Intelligence Unit.

Granstrand, Ove. 1999. *The Economics and Management of Intellectual Property: Towards Intellectual Capitalism.* Cheltenham, UK: Edward Elgar.

Hansell, Saul. 2003. "Aiming at Pornography to Hit Music Piracy," *The New York Times*. September 7, p.1. At: http://www.lexisnexis.com/universe (accessed 12 December 2005).

Huang, Cary. 2006 "Innovation is key to growth, says legislator; Switch to knowledge based economy is imperative for sustainable development," *The South China Morning Post*, 12 September.

Lerner, Josh. 2002. "Patent Protection and Innovation over 150 Years," Working Paper no. 8977, National Bureau of Economic Research, at http://www.nber.org/papers/w8977 (accessed 8 March 2005).

Lessig, Lawrence. 2004. *Free Culture: How Big Media Uses Technology and the Law to Lock Down Culture and Control Creativity*. New York: The Penguin Press.

Ma, Xiao. 2006. "Opportunities abound for Beijing." *The China Daily*. 14 July, 5. At: http://www.chinadaily.com.cn/china/2006-07/14/content_641047.htm (accessed 5 February 2007).

Matthews, Duncan. 2002. *Globalizing Intellectual Property Rights: The TRIPs Agreement*. London: Routledge.

May, Christopher. 1998. "Thinking, Buying, Selling: Intellectual Property Rights in Political Economy," *New Political Economy*, Vol. 3, No. 1, pp 59-78.

Mertha, Andrew. 2005. *The Politics of Piracy: Intellectual Property in Contemporary China*. Ithaca, NY: Cornell University Press.

Motion Picture Association of America (MPAA). 2004. *Anti-piracy: Regional Overviews: Asia/Pacific* At http://www.mpaa.org/anti-piracy/index.htm (accessed 8 March 2005).

National Copyright Administration of the People's Republic of China. 2004. *Enhance the Protection of Intellectual Property Rights and Intensify the Strength of Fighting Against the Infringement and Piracy: The Recent Situation of the Copyright Protection in China*, September 6. At http://www.china.org.cn/e-news/news040906-3.htm (accessed 27 May 2006).

Renmin Ri Bao, The People's Daily. 2006. "'*Fan daoban bai ri xingdong' jiebao pin chuan*, (The 100 Day Campaign Against Pirated Discs' Wins a series of victories.)," 20 October, 2006. at: http://culture.people.com.cn/GB/22219/4937911.html (accessed 5 February 2007).

Rosen, Hilary. 2003. "Effects and Consequences of an Emerging China," *Prepared Testimony of Chairman and CEO of RIAA, Subcommittee on East Asian and Pacific Affairs Committee on Foreign Relations, United States Senate*. At http://www.riaa.com/news/newsletter/031903_2.asp (accessed 15 March 2006).

Strathern, Marilyn. 1999. *Property, Substance and Effect: Anthropological Essays on Persons and Things*. London: The Athlone Press.

Tanner, Murray Scott. 2005. "Campaign-Style Policing in China and its Critics," in Børge Bakken (ed.), *Crime, Punishment, and Policing in China*, pp. 171-189. Lanham, MD: Rowman and Littlefield Publishers.

Vaidhyanathan, Siva. 2001. *Copyrights and Copywrongs: The Rise of Intellectual Property and How it Threatens Creativity*. New York: New York University Press.

Part IV

Community Perseverance

CHAPTER SEVEN

SHORELINE PROTECTION AND MANGROVES: A POST-TSUNAMI COMMUNITY ASSESSMENT IN SOUTHERN SRI LANKA*

RUSYAN JILL MAMIIT-COBURN
AND KAUSHALYA WIJAYAWEERA

Mangroves and Tsunami in Sri Lanka

Mangrove ecosystems inhabit in the brackish water margin between land and sea in most tropical and sub-tropical regions (Spaninks and van Beukering 1997). In Sri Lanka, 12,000 hectares of mangrove ecosystem (Pemadasa 1984) and 23 mangrove species (WRI 2003) populate 22 brackish water bodies, locally known as lagoons (WRM 1999). The most dominant mangrove species include *Rhizophora mucronata, Bruguiera gymnorhiza, Aegiceras corniculata R. apiculata, Cerebera manghas* and *Lumnitzera racemosa.* These species provide essential timber and non-timber products for domestic and commercial uses. Households around the mangrove areas use *Cerebera manghas* in making paper, matchsticks, household utensils, agricultural implements, toys and masks for many traditional cultural activities (AIMS 2005). Sri Lankans use mangrove tannin in curing fishnets. Twigs and branches of *Rhizophora mucronata, R. apiculata* and *Lumnitzera racemosa* provide materials to form "brush

---

* This study would have not been possible if not for the generous financial and professional support provided by the members of the IUCN Regional Ecosystems and Livelihood Groups-Sri Lanka and the IUCN Country Office-Sri Lanka. The authors are especially grateful to Lucy Emerton, Mikkel Kallesoe, Usman Iftikhar and Shamen Vidanage for initially developing the topic for the study. Equal gratitude is given to Kumi Ekarathne and Diana Alwis for the field assistance. The authors are also grateful to Sandun Perera, Gayathri Sriskanthan and Mattias Rust for the assistance in the reconnaissance survey.

piles" or "brush parks" in a specially devised fishing method in Sri Lanka (AIMS 2005). Mangrove lagoons supply the immediate seafood needs of approximately 120,000 residents in Sri Lanka's southwestern coastal belt (Pemadasa 1984). Apart from these goods, mangroves also provide ecological and environmental services such as storm and shoreline protection and stabilization, and control of soil erosion and flooding. Because of the wide array of goods and services it offers, Mitsch and Gosselink (1993) dubbed mangroves as "biological and economic supermarkets."

Similar to other natural ecosystems, mangroves in Sri Lanka have been exposed to both anthropogenic and naturally-induced interventions. The increased migration to coastal regions since Sri Lanka's independence in 1948 resulted in degradation of Sri Lanka's coastal vegetation, particularly mangroves (Global Oceans 2005). The World Rainforest Movement (1999) disclosed that many of the lagoons and estuaries in Sri Lanka have been subjected to rapid destruction of its mangrove vegetation for tourism and commercial aquaculture (Liyanage 1995). The intensification and rapid expansion of prawn farming on the west coast of Sri Lanka contributed to the conversion and subsequent decline of mangroves. The inadequacy and lack of implementation of governing mechanisms to regulate the use of the coastal and marine resources exacerbated the conditions of mangroves specifically in the southern Sri Lankan coast. In December 2004, mangroves in the southeastern coastal belt of Sri Lanka sustained severe damage caused by the tsunami that hit the Indian Ocean. The impact of the tsunami magnified the significance of the role of mangroves in the event of natural disasters such as a tsunami.

The 2004 Indian Ocean tsunami catastrophically demonstrated the long overlooked functions and services of mangrove ecosystems such as shoreline protection and stabilization, and flood and flow control. Anecdotal evidences and initial observations following the tsunami indicate that the existence of healthy mangroves helped reduce the destructive impacts of the tsunami in two ways: (i) dense mangrove forests offered resistance from speeding water and tidal waves to reach inland areas and (ii) the existence of natural water funnels in the mangrove ecosystem distributed the volume of tidal water, which in turn lowered the impact in inland settled areas (IEMA 2005 and MAP 2005).

In recognition of the need to better understand the protective role of mangrove ecosystems in mitigating the impacts of the tsunami, this study presents an assessment of the community perspectives on the shoreline protection function of mangroves in the villages of Kapuhenwala and Wanduruppa. This study reports the findings of the socioeconomic household surveys in two villages in southern Sri Lanka. The study also includes a comparative assessment of the damages sustained by a village identified with healthy and intact mangrove ecosystems versus a village identified with degraded mangroves prior to the tsunami.

Community Sites

With the intention of comparing the role of intact and degraded mangrove ecosystems in reducing the impacts of the tsunami, the reconnaissance site survey resulted in the selection of two sites with different mangrove resource endowments. The village of Kapuhenwala represents the area with healthy and intact mangrove ecosystem before the tsunami struck Sri Lanka, whereas, disturbed and degraded mangroves characterize the village of Wanduruppa. Located in the divisions of Tangalle and Ambalantota within the district of Hambantota, the two villages display a diversity of marine and coastal resources. The dominant natural vegetation includes mangroves, scrublands, salt marshes, reed beds and grasslands.

Kapuhenwala

Estuarine and deltaic coastlines characterize the village of Kapuhenwala. The major resources in Kapuhenwala upon which its 59 households depend for livelihood include farming and fisheries. Residents in Kapuhenwala have an average monthly household income of SLR5,000 (US$50).

Tourism has also been an important part of the village economy for the last decade. The mangrove ecosystems within the village represent 14 species. These include *Lumnitzera racemosa, Ceriops tagal, Avicenniaofficinalis, Sonneratia, Excoecaria agallocha, Bruguiera gymnorhiza, Rhizophora mucronata, Aegiceras corniculata* (Wijayaweera 2005). The village has one of the most abundant and intact mangrove ecosystems in southern Sri Lanka.

Following the Indian Ocean tsunami, anecdotal reports showed that the impact of the tsunami in Kapuhenwala was observed to have gone beyond 350 meters from the shoreline. This explains the massive destruction in most of the mangrove areas and human settlements next to the lagoon. The tsunami partially and totally destroyed a total of fifty houses in Kapuhenwala (Jeewananda 2005). Despite the degree of property destruction, the village of Kapuhenwala had the lowest number of fatalities with only two casualties recorded from the tsunami.

Wanduruppa

As a progressively growing community, the village of Wanduruppa has 512 households who depend on fishing and farming. Compared to other villages in Hambantota, Wanduruppa has a higher living standard with 41 percent of the households receiving an average monthly income of SLR7,500 (US$75). The availability of small cottage industries contributes to the average monthly household income in Wanduruppa.

The village of Wanduruppa has 34 hectares of agricultural lands. The Indian Ocean tsunami of 2004 severely damaged agricultural and fishery in the village. The tsunami destroyed 25 of the 26 beach seine nets used by the villagers for fishing (De Silva 2005). The disaster also impacted the crown-shaped patches of mangroves in Wanduruppa, which prior to the tsunami have been exposed to considerable human intervention and land conversion. The mangrove area starts from Walipatanwila and extends to Godawaya, covering an average area of 76 hectares. The dominant mangrove stands affected by the tsunami include *Sonneratia*, *Acrosticum aureum*, *Aegiceras corniculata*, *Acanthus illicifolius*, *Avicennia officinalis* (Wijayaweera 2005).

Socioeconomic Community Survey

To understand the community context concerning the role of mangroves in reducing the impact of the tsunami and compare the degree of damages of sites characterized with healthy and intact mangroves versus disturbed mangrove sites, the project team carried out household-based community surveys in the villages of Kapuhenwala and Wanduruppa. The selection of the household samples followed the purposive sampling approach (Robson 2002). Purposive sampling is used in quantitative social research in which a targeted sample needs to be reached quickly with less regard to random selection process or proportionality. By following such approach, the survey had 44 respondents out of 59 households in Kapuhenwala and 107 respondents out of 512 households in Wanduruppa.

The survey, which was carried out in English and Sinhala over a period of 10 days in April 2005, included questions on the assessment of the conditions and perceived role(s) of the mangroves in the communities, before and after the tsunami. Mangroves act as a natural barrier to waves coming inland. They help reduce the effects of storm surges and flooding. In light of better understanding the protective role of mangroves, the survey gathered information on the degree and amount of damages sustained by each household during the tsunami. The survey gave the respondents the opportunity to provide anecdotal evidence on the shoreline protection services of mangroves during the tsunami. It also covered questions related to each household's mangrove dependence and questions on property damages and loss economic activities.

The survey also included a section on issues related to resource governance, management options and the inclusion of mangrove rehabilitation efforts in the tsunami reconstruction and rebuilding process. The survey also obtained relevant socioeconomic and demographic information, both in the community and individual levels.

Sociodemographic Profile

The division of Tangalle has an estimated population of 62,800 from the 2001 census count and the division of Ambalantota has an estimated population of 64,361 (Department of Census and Statistics 2005). The village of Kapuhenwala belongs to the larger division of Tangalle and Wanduruppa belongs to Ambalantota. According to the 2001 census, Kapuhenwala and Wanduruppa have an average household size of four members. Buddhist Sinhalese dominate ninety-seven percent of the population in the two villages.

Nuclear family households dominate Kapuhenwala and Wanduruppa. The two villages have middle-aged population with 67 percent of the households in Kapuhenwala and 61 percent of the residents in Wanduruppa fall into the following age brackets: 31-40 years old and 41-50 years old, respectively. This suggests that majority of the population are in the workforce.

Because the community survey targeted head of households, the results showed a high male to female ratio. Based on the survey results, males account for 86 percent of the villagers in Kapuhenwala and 71 percent in Wanduruppa. The records at the Department of Census and Statistics (2005), however, show that the division of Tangalle has 0.98 male to female ratio, whereas, the division of Ambalantota has 1.04 male to female ratio.

In Wanduruppa, household income has a positive correlation with the villager's educational attainment. The survey results show that 42 percent of the households enjoy relatively higher monthly cash income (SLR5,000 or approximately US$50) compared to neighboring villages. The proximity of Wanduruppa to the Ambalantota town and accessibility of private and public educational institutions in the area reflects the high proportion (71 percent) of residents with an average formal education of eight years and higher monthly cash income. On average, barely 47 percent of the residents in Kapuhenwala attained eight years of formal education. The high level of literacy in Wanduruppa manifested a high degree of participation and membership of 62 percent of the population in environmental organizations.

Mangrove Dependence

To establish the level of dependence on and awareness of mangrove ecosystems in the two villages, the survey queried the resident's familiarity with the resource. Follow up questions on the residents actual and perceived uses and services of mangroves to the community, before and after the tsunami, also helped assess the level of dependence of the two communities on mangroves. The residents also rated the conditions of the mangrove ecosystems surrounding their villages as either (1) healthy or intact mangroves or (2) disturbed or degraded mangroves.

The residents of Kapuhenwala have a good understanding of the coastal resources in the area as shown by almost 100 percent familiarity of the villagers to mangroves on both sites. When asked on how the residents will rate the conditions of mangroves before the tsunami hit, 82 percent of the residents in Kapuhenwala agree that mangroves in the area were in intact and in healthy condition. Ninety percent of the residents in Kapuhenwala recognized the substantial devastation that the tsunami brought to the mangrove resources in their village.

In Wanduruppa, only 79 percent of the residents consider their mangroves as intact. The village elders in Wanduruppa expressed that 79 percent response rate overrates the actual condition of the mangroves surrounding the village. According to the elders, mangroves in Wanduruppa have been constantly hammered by anthropogenic activities and naturally induced events such as the constant flooding caused by the re-channeling of the river mouth in the village. The elders emphasized that mangroves in Wanduruppa are in very bad shape and the resident response does not reflect the degraded conditions of the resource.

Figure 7-1 Mangroves in Kapuhenwala

Figure 7-2 Mangroves in Wanduruppa

The residents in Kapuhenwala and Wanduruppa have identified mangroves as important source of fuel wood. The residents also recognized that mangroves serve as breeding grounds for fish. Prior to the tsunami, 52 percent of the residents engaged in mangrove fishing. Other mangrove services identified by the residents include: tourism, area for research and shoreline protection.

Figure 7-3 Fisherman engaged in mangrove fishing in Kapuhenwala

When asked to rank the different mangrove uses and services, the residents ranked the different mangrove functions as they perceived their importance and significance to their household, before the tsunami hit Sri Lanka and after the tsunami devastated their villages. In Kapuhenwala, residents feel that the most important function of mangroves before the tsunami is that mangroves are sources of fish. The residents hardly recognized the shoreline protection function of mangroves before the tsunami hit.

Table 7-1 Residents' ranking of the different mangrove uses and services in Kapuhenwala and Wanduruppa

Before the tsunami		Mangrove Uses and Services	After the tsunami	
Kap.*	Wan.**		Kap.*	Wan.**
4	6	Source of fuel wood	6	6
1	3	Source of fish	2	2
3	4	Recreational / tourist area	3	3
6	1	Protection from natural disasters (storms, tsunami)	1	1
5	2	Area for research	5	5
2	5	Nursery grounds for fish species	4	4

* Kap.: Kapuhenwala **Wan.: Wanduruppa

Interestingly, in Wanduruppa, before and after the tsunami, the residents have a good recognition of the role of mangroves as shoreline buffer during natural disasters such as a tsunami. The regular flooding caused by the re-channeling of the river mouth in Wanduruppa has influenced the hierarchical assignments of functions to mangroves. The ranking of respondents in Wanduruppa manifests that the shoreline protection and flood control functions of mangroves are of highest importance, before and after the tsunami. The residents in Kapuhenwala only realized the dominance of the protective role of mangroves after the tsunami.

Despite the high recognition for the protective function afforded by the mangrove ecosystems in Wanduruppa prior to the tsunami disaster, community members remained unresponsive to the incessant degradation of the mangroves in the area. The mangrove to population ratio, partly, explains why mangrove resources in Wanduruppa are more degraded despite the high recognition of the community of the different goods and services that can be derived from it. Wanduruppa has a narrower stretch of mangroves, which supports 512 households; whereas, Kapuhenwala has a broader and continuous strip of mangroves, which supports 59 households.

Village residents in Wanduruppa never imagined that anything worse than the frequent inundation that devastates the village could occur. The residents felt that the existing strip and patches of mangroves was sufficient to protect the village from flooding and other related disaster. After the tsunami, the residents in both villages admitted that by having the mangroves along the coast helped reduce the impact of tidal waves coming inland. Residents in Kapuhenwala mentioned that the mangroves prevented fatalities in their village. The villagers remembered that when they heard the waves coming, the waves hit the mangrove areas and slowed down, giving the residents enough time to go further inland. Kapuhenwala recorded the lowest number of fatalities among the villages in southern Sri Lanka with two casualties.

Mangroves and Tsunami Damages

Mangrove uses and services can be divided into direct and indirect use values. The provision of indirect support and protection to economic activity and property by the natural functions or regulatory "environmental" services consist the indirect use values associated with mangrove ecosystems (Spaninks and van Beukering 1997). The most unrecognized indirect services of mangroves include shoreline protection and flood control functions. The recent tsunami demonstrated these functions and generated interest among scholars on assessing the actual protective role of mangroves *i.e.,* buffer from storm damage, wave action and alluvial materials, at the event of natural disasters.

As part of the community survey, the residents provided their anecdotal experiences of the tsunami and perception on the actual role(s) of the mangroves during the tsunami. Residents from both Kapuhenwala and Wanduruppa articulated that the mangroves were able to reduce the impacts of waves coming inland. Ninety-five percent of the villagers in Kapuhenwala recognized the shoreline protection function of the mangroves during the tsunami; whereas only 85 percent of the households in Wanduruppa acknowledged the service. Residents in Wanduruppa felt that the patches of narrow stretch of mangroves in Wanduruppa were not able to offer as much protection compared to broader and continuous stretch of mangroves in Kapuhenwala. According to 85 percent of the residents in Wanduruppa and 98 percent of the villagers in Kapuhenwala, damages to infrastructure and properties as well as casualties would have been more substantial if there are no mangroves surrounding the villages.

Figure 7-4 illustrates the degree of damages on both sites. Early tsunami reports assessed that 68 percent of the houses in Wanduruppa were damaged (De Silva 2005). The study survey, however, revealed that by considering fully damaged, partially damaged (unusable) and partially damaged (usable) structures as "damaged," 90 percent of houses in Wanduruppa were actually damaged by the tsunami. The village of Wanduruppa registered greater percentage of damages compared to Kapuhenwala. This confirms the initial claims and immediate observations after the tsunami that areas with broader mangroves parallel to the coasts experienced relatively lesser damages than areas with more disturbed mangrove ecosystems. Interestingly, Kapuhenwala had greater boat and fishing gear loss. The villagers explained that fishermen in Kapuhenwala leave their boats and gears along the coast after their daily fishing activities, and this made the boats and fishing gears more vulnerable to the impact of the tidal waves.

Previous studies, which investigated the shoreline protection function of mangroves, have assessed the function based on expected property and livelihood damages or expenditures on preventing such damage from taking place. Existing literature that assessed the shoreline protection services of mangroves have either used the replacement cost approach or preventive expenditure approaches (Bann 1997, Emerton 1998, Sathirathai and Barbier 2001, Spurgeon 2002, and Hirway and Goswami 2004) to ascertain the economic value of shoreline protection services of mangroves. This study used actual damage estimates and employed the damage cost avoided approach to assess damages on private properties, livelihood and public infrastructure from two sites severely affected by the tsunami. Actual damage estimates are cost estimates generated through the household survey. The term actual implies that the damage estimates used in the analysis were not an extrapolation of cost estimates from other locations hit by disasters of similar magnitude.

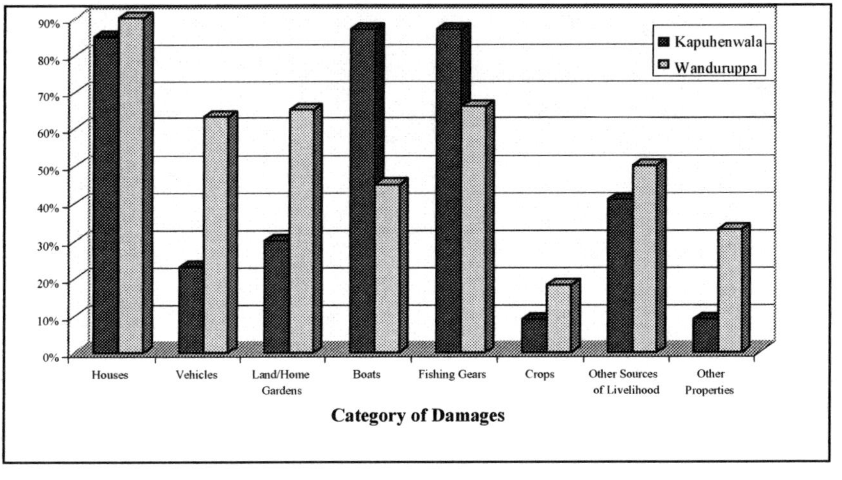

Figure 7-4 Percentage of households who experienced damages on their properties and livelihood.

The damage cost approach generated the costs of property damages in Kapuhenwala and Wanduruppa. Properties include houses, vehicles, hotels and residential lands. The damage to livelihood includes destruction of fishing gears, boats and crops. The costs of damage to community infrastructure include damage costs on public roads, schools, causeways and public parks. Based on the proportion of houses damaged on each site and the number of households engaged to either fishing or farming, the damage cost analysis derived an adjusted property damage value for the two villages. Table 7-2 summarizes the damages incurred in the study sites.

The estimates show that the costs of property damages in Wanduruppa, the village with degraded mangroves is more than ten times the costs of property damages in Kapuhenwala, the village with healthy and intact mangrove ecosystem. The damage cost estimates confirms the initial conjecture that the degree and amount of destruction is greater in areas where mangrove ecosystem is more degraded. The residents in both villages believe that Kapuhenwala had the lower damage costs and number of casualties from the tsunami, primarily, because of the healthy and intact mangrove ecosystems surrounding the village's shoreline.

Table 7-2 Costs of tsunami damages to property and livelihood in Kapuhenwala and Wanduruppa

Damages	**Total Weighted Costs (in SLR)**		**Damage Costs Avoided (SLR/household)**
	Kapuhenwala	***Wanduruppa***	
Property	SLR6,666,750 (US$66,668)	SLR116,136,395 (US$1,161,364)	SLR191,716 (US$1,917)
Livelihood	SLR8,676,092 (US$86,761)	SLR19,952,467 (US$199,525)	SLR19,748 (US$197)
Community Infrastructure	SLR1,980,000 (US$19,800)	SLR1,700,000 (US$17,000)	(SLR490) (-US$5)
Others (*e.g.*, Appliances, Clothes, etc.)	SLR32,625 (US$326)	SLR8,594 (US$86)	(SLR42) (-US$.50)
Total	SLR17,355,467 (US$173,555)	SLR137,797,456 (US$1,377,975)	SLR210,932 (US$2,109)

* Exchange rate in May 2005: US$ 1 = SLR 100.

The damage cost avoided estimates were adjusted based on the number of households affected on each site, size of coastal area with stretch of mangroves (healthy or disturbed), and value of damages generated by each household from each site. Table 7-2 shows the amount of damages or costs that could have been avoided had Wanduruppa had the same quality and conditions of mangrove ecosystems along its coastline as that of Kapuhenwala. The estimates, which were derived by calculating the difference between the monetary values of the damages on both sites, underscore the significant role of intact and healthy mangroves in the event of disasters such as a tsunami. It suggests that had Kapuhenwala had the same quality or condition of mangroves as that of Wanduruppa, it would have incurred an additional damage cost of SLR210,932 per household (US$2,109/household). These damage cost avoided estimates, therefore, can be translated as the total monetary value of the shoreline protection function of intact mangrove ecosystems.

Post-Tsunami Mangrove Rehabilitation

The Indian Ocean tsunami had major effects not only on coastal villages but ecosystems as well. An assessment of coastal villages after the tsunami shows that villages endowed with rich coastal vegetation such as mangroves and beach forests sustained far less damage than areas without such ecosystems. In Kapuhenwala, for instance, early tsunami reports revealed that mangroves helped provide protection and reduce effects on the community. In Wanduruppa, on the other hand, mangroves and other coastal vegetation have been cleared or degraded along the coastline, which increased the village's vulnerability to flood and tsunami damage.

The rehabilitation of mangrove areas and other coastal forests in the two villages and other coastal villages of Sri Lanka may play a key role in reducing the effect of future catastrophic events such as tsunami. For these reasons, mangrove rehabilitation should be an important part of the post-tsunami rehabilitation process. Residents in both Kapuhenwala and Wanduruppa agree that mangrove rehabilitation efforts should be an integral part of the tsunami reconstruction and rebuilding plans. Ninety-five percent of the villagers in both sites expressed their willingness to participate on ongoing and future mangrove rehabilitation efforts, mostly by volunteering their time and labor.

Conclusion

The recent tsunami that hit the island state of Sri Lanka damaged many properties and infrastructure. The disaster brought devastation to the natural marine and coastal vegetation upon which most coastal residents depend for food and livelihood. The protective role of mangrove ecosystems was substantially and tragically demonstrated by the Indian Ocean tsunami. Findings from the community survey corroborated theoretical claims on the role of healthy and intact mangroves as important tidal barrier against natural disasters such as tsunamis.

The findings demonstrate that damage costs for sites with healthy and intact mangroves are significantly lower compared to areas with disturbed ecosystems. The results of the damage costs avoided assessment for the shoreline protection function of mangroves provide a sound basis for the inclusion of mangrove rehabilitation efforts in the post-tsunami reconstruction and rebuilding efforts. The estimate suggests that mangroves, if managed sustainably, represent a much higher overall community benefit.

The absence of incentive tools to effectively manage mangrove resources in Sri Lanka send an alarming signal on the future of the remaining mangroves ecosystems in the country. This calls for a strengthened institutional framework to implement mangrove management tools such as land-use planning and economic incentives to promote sustainable use of the mangrove resources.

Works Cited

AIMS. 2005. *The Use of Mangroves*. http://www.aims.gov.au/pages/research/mangroves/mangrove-uses.html (accessed on 14 March 2005).

Bann, C. 1997. *The Economic Valuation of Mangroves: A Manual for Researchers*. Ottawa, Canada: International Development Research Centre.

De Silva, J. 2005. President, Pradeshiya Sabha of Ambalantota and GN of Waduruppa North. *Personal Communication*. 20 April. Ambalantota, Hambantota, Sri Lanka.

Department of Census and Statistics. 2005. *http://www.statistics.gov.lk/* (accessed on 11 March 2005).

Emerton, L. 1998. *Economic Tools for Valuing Wetlands in Eastern Africa*. IUCN: Africa.

Global Oceans. 2005. *Sri Lanka ICM Country Profile*.

http://www.globaloceans.org/country/srilanka/srilanka.html (accessed on 14 March 2005).

Hirway, I and S. Goswami. 2004. *Valuation of Mangroves in Gujarat*. India: Centre for Development Alternatives.

IEMA. 2005. *IEMA News*. http://www.iema.net/article.php?sid=3609 (accessed on 14 March 2005).

Jeewananda, R. 2005. Grama Niladari of Medilla. *Personal Communication*. 5 April. Medilla, Tangalle, Sri Lanka.

Liyanage, S. 1995. *Pilot Project on Participatory Management of Seguwanthive Mangrove Habitat in Puttalam District of Sri Lanka*. Paper presented to the International Conference on Wetlands and Development, 8-14 October 1995, Selangor, Malaysia.

MAP. 2005. *Mangrove Action Project*. http://www.earthisland.org/map/tsunami.htm#1 (accessed on 14 March 2005).

Mitsch, W and J. Gosselink. 1993. *Wetlands*. New York: Van Nostrand Reinhold, 2nd Edition.

Pemadasa, M. 1984. "Grasslands," in C.H. Fernando, (ed.), *Ecology and biogeography in Sri Lanka*. The Hague, The Netherlands: W Junk Publishers, pp. 99–131.

Robson, C. 2002. *Real World Research: A Resource for Social Scientists and Practitioner-Researchers*. New York: Blackwell Publishing Limited.

Sathirathai, S and E. Barbier. 2001. "Valuing Mangrove Conservation in Southern Thailand," *Contemporary Economic Policy*, Vol. 19, No. 2, 2001, pp 109-122.

Spaninks, F and P. van Beukering. 1997. *Economic Valuation of Mangroves: A Review of Techniques and Case Studies with Special Attention to the Production Function Approach*. London: CREED Working Paper Series. IIED.

Spurgeon, J. 2002. *Socioeconomic Assessment and Economic Valuation of Egypt's Mangroves*. Cairo: FAO, United Nations.

Wijayaweera, K. 2005. IUCN Staff. *Personal Communication*. 5 April. Colombo, Sri Lanka.

WRI. 2003. *Earth Trends: The Environmental Information Portal*. http://earthtrends.wri.org (accessed on 15 March 2005).

WRM. 1999. *Local Fisherfolk Protect the Mangroves in Sri Lanka*. http://www.wrm.org.uy/ bulletin/20/SriLanka.html (accessed on 15 March 2005).

CHAPTER EIGHT

TRADITIONAL INSIGHTS FOR SUSTAINABLE WOMEN EMPOWERMENT PROCESS IN A DISADVANTAGED COMMUNITY IN THE SOUTH OF VIETNAM

HUONG TRAN

Primary Health Care in Vietnam

With reformation initiated in the mid-1980s, Vietnam accepted a market economy and focused its efforts on developing the country. This however, increased disparity between the rich and the poor. Government statistics reported that the gap between the rich and poor was 4.1 times in 1995, seven times in 2000 and 8.1 times in 2003.[1] The gap in health care for those at different economic levels was even larger, especially between the delta and the mountainous areas. "Health for all" became a crucial challenge, not only for the government but also for development agencies.

Since 1985, Primary Health Care (PHC)[2] has been officially mentioned in health policies of the Vietnamese government.[3] All of the national vertical health programs[4] such as the Expanded Program on Immunization,

---

[1] Statistics from the Vietnamese Ministry of Finance's website 2005.

[2] "Primary Health Care is essential health care based on practical, scientifically sound and socially acceptable methods and technology made universally accessible to individuals and families in the community through their full participation and at a cost that the community and the country can afford to maintain at every stage of their development in the spirit of self-determination," defined according to the Conference Alma Ata, 1978, organized by the WHO and the UNICEF.

[3] Source: "Strategic Planning for time frame 1986-1990," Vietnamese Ministry of Health.

[4] National vertical health programs: the programs that are controlled by national institutions or ministries all over the country.

Control of Diarrhea Diseases, Nutrition Rehabilitation, Malaria Control and Acute Respiratory Infection have been implemented mainly through health systems with the coordination of mass organizations at all levels. Most of these programs were supported by UN agencies and international NGOs with contribution from the Vietnamese government. In recent years, the government has allocated more funds for PHC, which includes strengthening the health network at a basic level.

In Vietnam, the health system was established from the central level to provinces, districts and communes.[5] At the lowest level, there was a commune health center, which consisted of four to five health workers. These health workers were in charge of implementing all health programs for about 1,200-1,500 households. However the existence of separate hamlets and transportation difficulties prevented staff members from catering to the 5,000-8,000 inhabitants.[6] To carry out these programs, commune health workers tried to set up a PHC network, which was composed of village health workers, and cadres of mass organizations at the village level. The presence of mass organizations such as the Youth Union, Women's Union and Farmer's Union strengthened the system. Unfortunately, these local and national organizations that were under the guidance of the Communist Party usually conducted their activities in a top-down manner. As a result, the cadres of mass organization at the basic level hardly mobilized community participation.

Several development projects supported by international NGOs explored methods to enhance community participation and empower marginalized people. A key issue for sustainability was involving a person from the community.

Social Norms Relating to Empowerment and Participation

Vietnamese culture is strongly influenced by Confucianism[7] and Buddhism. A sense of community service prevails, particularly in the rural

---

[5] Under the Vietnamese administrative structure, each province consists of five to ten districts. Each district, in turn, is composed of 15 to 25 communes. A commune is the official way to refer to a village.

[6] Data from annual reports of the provincial health departments.

[7] Confucian ethical teaching includes the following values: ***Li***: includes ritual, propriety, etiquette, etc.; ***Hsiao***: love within the family: love of parents for their children and of children for their parents; ***Yi***: righteousness; ***Xin***: honesty and trustworthiness; ***Yen***: benevolence, humaneness towards others; the highest Confucian virtue; ***Chung***: loyalty to the state, etc (source: http://www.religioustolerance.org/confuciu.htm)

areas with everyone involved in community development on a voluntary basis. Each member's contribution is recognized as the contribution of the whole family. There is a sense of honor in helping disadvantaged people, including non-relatives. Supporting vulnerable people is considered a human value even when people themselves are suffering hardships. The following proverb reflected this values *"If you don't act when facing the righteousness you are not a hero."* While economic development has had an effect on these cultural traditions, most rural communities are still guided by the principles of community service.

Project in Tan Hung Commune

Tan Hung is one of the poorest communes of the Binh Phuoc province in South Vietnam, located in a mountainous area, 20 kilometers away from the highway. Tan Hung consists of five villages with 918 households. The Kinh made up 50 percent of the 3,760 inhabitants, while the rest are ethnic minority groups, which include the Tay, Nung, Chau Ro and Stieng. Household poverty rates are at 14 percent.

Most villagers earn income mainly through farming on hill lands, with cashews being the key crop. Farming is supplemented with cassava and sweet potato, and forest products such as bamboo shoots, honey and wood are also collected. About 60 percent of the households are involved in animal husbandry.[8]

The ethnic minority groups however, have a lower income due to a lack of funding to invest in agriculture. Language barriers also result in them being marginalized from social-economic development policies. Illiteracy was at 20 percent and most villagers had limited education.

The remoteness of this mountainous commune is further heightened by poor roads. It takes one hour to reach the closest village from the center. Inter-village roads are slopping pathways which become muddy and slippery during the rainy season and dusty in the dry season.

One of the difficulties villagers faced was the lack of an effective health care system. The location of the commune health center made it inaccessible to villagers in remote hamlets. The percentage of home birth was at 45 percent (survey report in 2002). About 63 percent of all pregnant women did not receive proper prenatal care. Other health problems include lack of access to safe water and sanitation facilities, and malnutrition in

---

[8] All social and health-related data about Binh Phuoc province and Tan Hung commune was extracted from results of the nutrition status survey conducted by Nutrition Center of Ho Chi Minh City, 2002.

children under five years old. A survey conducted by the Nutrition Center of Ho Chi Minh City reported that the prevalence of malnutrition in children under five years old was 35 percent overall and up to 45 percent in minority groups (survey report in 2002). Commune health workers who were not adequately trained in community approaches only went to the villages on immunization days. These health workers assigned by local authorities, implemented the vertical national programs, without participation from the villagers.

However since 2003, the Nutrition Center of Ho Chi Minh City has implemented a community-based Nutrition Rehabilitation Project in order to mobilize the participation of the community in Tan Hung to solve the malnutrition problem. This project established a volunteer network to empower villagers in health promotion at the grassroots level.

This chapter concentrates on the traditional and cultural motives that enable and enhance the volunteer network in the Tan Hung commune, and also on the role of incentives in community participation. Data collection was carried out using qualitative methods, with in-depth interviews and focus group discussions being key tools. Secondary data sources included volunteer meeting minutes and project reports. The study found that real participation and an empowerment process through the establishment and implementation of volunteer networks were the key factors in its sustainability and efficacy.

Volunteer Selection: Utilizing a Participatory Approach

In June 2003, a volunteer network consisting of 25 women was established. The villagers selected the volunteers through village meetings, with half of the volunteers coming from ethnic minority groups. Most of the volunteers were regular villagers and only a few held government positions, such as head of the Women Union (WU) in the village and chairperson of the commune Population Committee. The villagers were directly involved in the selection process of nominating and voting on their chosen volunteers. This process was empowering to the volunteers selected as it demonstrated the trust the community placed in them. As Mrs. Vui, a volunteer from Cay Cay village expressed, "We must work hard to take care of mothers and children because the villagers trusted us and voted us in." Mrs. Dao, another volunteer, emphasized, "When the villagers believed in my capacity, I felt I had to be responsible for their health."

The participation process was particularly empowering to ethnic minority volunteers as it inferred a strong sense of acceptance by the community. These volunteers were provided a space to share their experiences which assisted in building up self-confidence, and enable them to express their needs and solutions. Mrs. Huong, an ethnic minority from the Chau Ro community, cried with happiness and said,

> "Before the project I never believed that I was accepted and recognized by the group. Today my opinions are really appreciated by people, so I am very happy."

Empowerment through Effective Training

For two years, volunteers attended successive workshops that upgraded their understanding of PHC and improved their skills, especially in communication and project management. The official workshops were as follows:

- Maternal and child health care, including nutrition
- Communication skills for individual and community groups
- Participatory planning, monitoring and evaluation
- Water supply and environment sanitation
- Meeting facilitation skills
- Group-formation and building skills

The training contents were selective and relevant to the community, and applied a participatory learning approach. This enabled volunteers to take an active role in the learning process where their experiences were used as the starting point for each session.

All volunteers appreciated this learning experience which not only provided them with practical knowledge and skills, but also conferred them a status of prestige in their community. Mrs. Lan, a volunteer in the Pa Pech village, thought that group-building skills "were extremely useful in terms of capacity building." Mrs. Sam concluded that because of the trainings, network members understood and supported each other.

Providing a Sense of Ownership

The project began with building long-term goals, a process which involved the volunteers. Volunteers drew a picture of the commune based on a future where people would lead comfortable and self-reliant lives. They outlined the results expected in two years and the specific activities needed to be carried out. They developed a deeper insight on their impact of their contribution to the community through their daily activities. Mrs. Vinh, the head of network, reported, "We understand well why we focused our efforts on improving the health care knowledge and skills of our women."

In contrast to the regular pattern of the annual plan for vertical health programs be set by higher level officials (e.g. district Health Office), the volunteers in the Tan Hung project were actively involved in the annual, quarterly and monthly planning of the health programs with the facilitation of project staff. Participatory planning not only helped volunteers understand project implementation but also provided volunteers a sense ownership over the project. Also in contrast to meetings in other communes which were always chaired by the head of the Commune Health Center or chairman of the Population Committee, volunteers in the Tan Hung project rotated in facilitating the village monthly meetings. This enabled for active participation of the network members and incorporated a further sense of ownership. As said by one volunteer, "We felt that we were implementing our project instead of the project of the Nutrition Center."

Although the project had identified the volunteers' role as being a bridge between villagers and the commune health center, volunteers were provided an opportunity to clarify their specific responsibilities during the first meeting. This assisted in preventing a feeling of being imposed on. All volunteers could list their tasks, which included collecting health-related data, participating in the planning process, communicating with household and women's groups, conducting monthly weight check-ups for children, giving a cooking demonstration to the village, attending training provided by the project, and preparing a monthly report. Each volunteer took between eight to ten days to accomplish her work. During the two-year period, most volunteers consistently conducted their activities irrespective of bad weather, poor transportation system and the indifferent attitudes of some villagers.

The volunteers' work produced excellent results. A regular activity was teaching mothers to prepare a nutritional meal for children under five. Although the initially attraction towards this program was the free meal provided to children, mothers continued with this program out of interest. The nutritious foods used in this activity were cheap or easily available from the backyard garden. Most of the mothers practiced and provided positive feedback on these meals, stating that their children enjoyed the food and steadily gained weight. The mothers were also provided instruction on breast feeding, immunization, acute respiratory infection and nutrition. A participant stated that, "for hundred years, we had done things the same way. This is the first time we have learned that pregnant women need to take care of themselves and have learnt how to do it."

Approximately 80 percent of pregnant women went for health-checkups and the percentage of delivery at the health center increased to 81 percent. These results provided a huge source of motivation and encouragement to the volunteers.

The volunteers were also involved in many other health care and community activities. Volunteers helped villagers hold community meetings to discuss and solve village-level problems. These meetings led to the construction of a water tower in the commune center by the villagers. Within six months, 53 households were motivated into building water containers. This significantly reduced the hardship of women in accessing clean water. The project also supported the building of a latrine, and by the end of December 2005, 67 households had built their latrine.

The attendance at the monthly volunteer meetings was surprisingly high (more than 80 percent) in comparison with similar meetings in this commune. Data was reported and monitored based on a quarterly plan. There was clear evidence that the volunteer network could be sustainable without outside support.

Table 8-1 Volunteer network of Tan Hung

Date	Number of members	Note
June 2003	25	
June 2004	18	7 members dropped out
June 2005	24	6 new members
Dec 2005	23	1 member dropped out

The Nutrition Rehabilitation project in Tan Hung was being phased out at the end of June 2005. Although the financial support was reduced to a minimal level, the volunteers still carried out the activities, mainly focusing on health communication. They also continued to work on rainwater jar collection and latrine construction. In order to cover the operational costs, the commune PMB reallocated funds from available sources. Mrs. Tam, a volunteer from the Cay Cay village, said, "We see no reason to stop working regardless of the project ending or not."

Acknowledgement from Local Authorities

Volunteers did not receive any direct financial incentives for their participation. This was a depart from government precedent in which village health workers were paid US$6 per month and population collaborators were paid US$2 per month. Financial remuneration paid to participants in other projects did not result in a higher level of commitment, with some networks collapsing or were ineffective. In fact, the incentives that were provided did not meet actual costs incurred for carrying out project duties.

Many volunteers felt hurt when asked how much they were paid for carrying out their duties, as they felt no amount of financial remuneration could motivate anyone from carrying out such a difficult task.

However in order to honor their work rather than to "pay" them, volunteers were provided non-financial initiatives. Volunteers were exempted from annual labor duty and their children received a tuition fee remission. Although health insurance was not popular, volunteers were provided with free treatment at the commune health center when they became ill. Volunteers also received priority in some economic activities such as borrowing loans.

Recognition and Support from Family Members and the Community

The participation of women in this project challenged the established gender roles, that the presence of women in public affairs was not encouraged. The support provided by their husbands was crucial in enabling the women volunteers carry out their duties. The commune PMB and project staff spent time explaining each volunteer's dedication to the community, to their family members.

The support of the husbands was clearly seen though their willingness to manage the housework such as cooking, washing and animal feeding while their wives attended training in Ho Chi Minh City that took them 150 km from their native commune. Most of the husbands continued with the housework so that their wives could undertake home visits and attend group meetings. It was said that 90 percent of the husbands highly appreciated the meaningful contribution of their wives. The support of the husbands could also be seen through their willingness to bring them for monthly meetings at the commune centre. Mr. Doan, a volunteer's husband in a remote village said that he felt happy to drive his wife to the meetings because he knew that "my wife was respected by villagers."

The recognition from the larger community was also emotionally rewarding for volunteers. A Volunteer's Festival was held at the end of second year, to provide an opportunity to the community to recognize the efforts of the volunteers. The event was attended by government officials who expressed a formal acknowledgment of appreciation.

Conclusion

The findings of this study suggest that commitment towards a project is depended significantly upon participatory approaches rather than on incentives. In the Tan Hung commune, volunteers were actively involved from the beginning of the project. This provided a sense of ownership and responsibility. Being valued by their families and community was a major source of encouragement. Maslow's theory explains that people have a human need to be useful to others even when they are still not so comfortable in their own basic needs. This principle can be applied in this case study, and is supported by Vietnamese social norms which encourages people to help others.

Therefore, to improve primary health care of disadvantaged communities in mountainous, remote and poorer areas, participation and empowerment of its community members are key factors. It is noted from this study that the deeper motivations that drive these volunteers are not the typical Western cultural notions of incentives and individual achievements. Rather, they are based on social norms and the love of their homeland and neighborhood, as well as the support from their husbands and families. The combination of a participatory approach in an empowerment process in conjunction with the traditional values of Vietnamese culture are important factors in sustaining project activities.

To set up a sustainable health network, it is suggested that all stakeholders be involved and taken seriously at all stages of the project. Participants also need to be empowered through training sessions and know that the community places its trust in them. Community spirit, the strength of love for the homeland and the characteristics of a local community should be considered as important social capital in such a network or project. Finally, officials need to incorporate into their policies ways of honoring these volunteers, rather than providing financial remuneration, in an effort to create a sustainable model.

Works Cited

Son, Nam. 1997. *Ca Tinh Mien Nam* (Characteristics of people of the South). Youth Publisher.

—. 1992. *Van Minh Miet Vuon* (Civilization of the Garden Country). Culture Publisher.

Nguyen, Dip V. 2000. *Tai lieu dao tao y te thon ban* (Training documents for rural health workers) – WHO, UNICEF.

Nutbeam, Don, 1998. *Health Promotion Glossary*. WHO.

Werner, David and Bill Bower. 1990. *Helping Health Workers Learn.*

Hubley, John. 1993. *Communicating Health*. The MacMillan Press Ltd.

Pham, Hung M., Lieu H. Duong, and Long H. Nguyen. 2002. *Health Policies and Guidelines*. Vietnam Medical Publisher.

Victor, Brigit W. and the research group of Danish Red Cross Office in Vietnam. 2000. *Village Volunteer network for Primary Health Care in Mekong Delta of Vietnam*. Vietnam Medical Publisher.

CHAPTER NINE

AFTER THE STORM OF 2000: FIJI'S TROUBLED PATH TOWARD JUSTICE AND RECONCILIATION[1]

KEVIN CHANG

The once sleepy and peaceful islands of Fiji have in recent decades experienced an unprecedented level of political and societal upheaval. As this chapter was being finalized, yet another *coup d'état*, Fiji's fourth, had taken place. On December 5, 2006, Commodore Frank Bainimarama, Commander of the Republic of Fiji Military Forces (RFMF), made true of his persistent threats to remove the government headed by Prime Minister Laisenia Qarase. Through a bloodless but forceful process of gradually strangulating Qarase and his ministers' capacity to govern, Bainimarama seized power under the justification that a coup was necessary to rid Fiji of the government's corrupt and racially discriminatory policies and practices.

This latest coup marks the fourth time in the past two decades that Fiji has experienced an overthrow of government. The genesis of Fiji's cycle of coups can be traced back to May 1987, when Lieutenant-Colonel Sitiveni Rabuka deposed by gunpoint the newly elected multiethnic government led by Prime Minister Timoci Bavadra in what was the first overthrow of government in the South Pacific region. Months later, Rabuka would execute a second coup to halt the process of establishing a transitional government that would guide the country back to democratic

[1] I would like to thank Dagny Margrete Fosen, Jone Dakuvula, James Deshaw Rae and Russell Daye for their valuable comments on an earlier version of this chapter. I would also like to thank the East-West Center, Hawai'i for encouraging and facilitating this chapter's publication. The views expressed in this chapter are those of the author and do not necessarily represent the views of the organizations he is affiliated with.

rule. History would repeat itself thirteen years later in May 2000, when a group fronted by George Speight executed a civilian takeover of parliament, deposing the democratically elected People's Coalition Government led by Mahendra Chaudhry, the country's first ever Indo-Fijian Prime Minister.[2]

Both the 1987 and 2000 coups were underpinned by indigenous Fijian ethnonationalism, with Speight and Rabuka professing to act selflessly in safeguarding indigenous Fijian political supremacy. In the wake of both events, the country was plunged into turmoil in the form of widespread racially motivated violence with long lasting political, social and economic consequences. This latest coup of December 2006 has been the culmination of open hostility between the military and the Qarase-led SDL[3] Coalition Government. But unlike previous coups, it has been absent of an overt racial motive. It may be still too early to conclude whether the current crisis will inflict a similar toll on Fiji's political, social and economic development as it experienced after the turmoil of 1987 and 2000. One thing however is certain—that Fiji has again returned to being ruled by the gun, the most fatal setback being its own democratic future.

In the aftermath of the 2000 coup, Fiji embarked on a process of national reconciliation in an attempt to heal the wounds of a fractured society and build a peaceful future. This chapter will analyze and assess Fiji's path towards reconciliation since the 2000 coup, focusing particularly on the attainment of justice through political, judicial and wider societal processes. Fiji's reconciliation process will be considered in the broader context of the country's struggles with democratization and its search for peaceful coexistence, and through this, the chapter will seek to explain how failure by Fiji's leaders to dispassionately confront issues from the past has contributed to the latest crisis. Finally, the chapter will outline some key issues that must be addressed for building sustainable peace in the islands.

---

[2] In this chapter, the term "indigenous Fijian" is used to refer to descendents of those residents in the islands prior to British arrival—including those from Melanesian, Polynesian and Micronesian ancestries. The term "Indo-Fijian" is used to refer to descendents of indentured laborers and free settlers who arrived from India in the late 19th and early 20th centuries. Note that within Fiji, the two groups are customarily referred to as "Fijian" and "Indian" respectively. Some indigenous Fijians believe that the term "Fijian" should be reserved exclusively for references to the indigenous population. This chapter will use the term "Fiji Islander" as a collective reference to the peoples of Fiji.

[3] *Soqosoqo Duavata ni Lewenivanua* (Fijian Unity Party).

The Context of Reconciliation after the 2000 Coup

The civilian coup of 19 May 2000 led by businessman George Speight again sank Fiji into deep political and social chaos. The militant indigenous nationalism that brought about the 1987 coup had resurfaced, and once again, a democratically elected multiethnic government was violently ousted under the banner of indigenous Fijian rights. The coup was a major setback to Fiji's decade-long effort to rebuild itself from the 1987 crisis through political consensus-building and democratization, highlighted by the promulgation of the 1997 Constitution. The Constitution restored equitable parliamentary representation for Fiji's main ethnic groups; provided a power-sharing arrangement among major political parties; and encouraged good governance and respect for human rights. It also sought to delicately preserve the paramountcy of indigenous Fijian interests[4] through reserving key government posts to indigenous Fijians and maintaining indigenous ownership of more than 80 percent of the country's land.[5]

Despite constitutional entrenchment of indigenous political supremacy and land ownership, the months leading up to the 2000 coup were marked by widespread fears among indigenous communities that the land reform policy proposed by the Chaudhry Government would severely impact upon their livelihood. Through fanning the latent fears of Indian domination, helped by Chaudhry's insensitive handling of an issue highly emotive to indigenous land owners, indigenous ethnonationalists were able to arouse racial fervor among its grassroots in calling for Chaudhry's resignation. Speight was the front man of a rebel group containing elements of the military[6] that answered the call, storming Parliament and holding Chaudhry and his coalition parliamentarians' hostage. Unlike

[4] The "paramountcy of (indigenous) Fijian interests" is a concept advocated by colonial rulers such that indigenous Fijian interests are to be protected and not subordinated under other groups (Lal 1992). In recent times, however, the concept has often been employed by indigenous nationalists in their calls for greater indigenous political supremacy.

[5] The 1997 Constitution confers significant powers to the Great Council of Chiefs, including its appointment of the President, the Vice President and 14 out of 32 Senators. The Constitution also reaffirms the colonial provisions that prohibited the alienation of native land. The Colonial Administration locked 83 percent of all land to indigenous clans (Reddy and Naidu 2001). The percentage of native land in the country has increased to around 90 percent of late due to the incorporation of unclaimed and government-purchased freehold land (Kurer 2001).

[6] The 2000 coup involved members from the Counter Revolutionary Warfare, an elite military unit established by Rabuka during the 1987 coup.

1987, however, Speight's group could not secure the support of critical indigenous Fijian establishments—President Ratu Sir Kamisese Mara, the Military, and the Great Council of Chiefs (GCC). As the military, led by Commander Frank Bainimarama, assumed executive authority over the country, it was locked in a power struggle with the rebels, whose supporters were by now rampaging towns and villages as lawlessness pervaded. The 56-day hostage crisis was eventually dissolved after the military acceded to most of Speight's demands in the Muanikau Accord.[7] When Speight and his rebels refused to surrender their ammunition, Bainimarama swiftly arrested the group and proceeded to install an Interim Government headed by Laisenia Qarase, an indigenous Fijian Senator who had fiercely opposed Chaudhry's land reform policies.

The 1987 and 2000 coups were both triggered by fervent, though largely misplaced, fears among many indigenous Fijians about the effects an Indo-Fijian dominated government would have on indigenous livelihood. These fears were aroused by indigenous ethnonationalists who equated indigenous rights to indigenous political supremacy, and argued that political leadership must always remain in the hands of indigenous Fijians.[8] Indigenous fears of Indo-Fijian domination persist despite the fact that indigenous Fijians have dominated Fiji's political leadership since independence, and that the Indo-Fijian population has been in rapid decline since the 1987 coup.[9] Political mobilization along ethnic lines has been a hallmark of Fiji's electoral contests, with most parties dominated by one ethnic group largely as a consequence of the country's ethnic-based parliamentary representative system.[10] Despite the fact that ethnicity has

---

[7] The demands from Speight's group included abrogation of the 1997 Constitution, dismissal of the Chaudhry Government, resignation of Ratu Sir Kamisese Mara as President, and the group's guaranteed immunity from prosecution (Robertson and Sutherland 2002).

[8] The cry "Fiji for (indigenous) Fijians" was a popular rallying point by indigenous ethno-nationalists in both 1987 and 2000. Qarase, as did indigenous Fijian political leaders before him, exploited the issue of race by declaring that indigenous Fijians are not ready to accept an Indo-Fijian Prime Minister (Fiji Times, August 3, 2004).

[9] For the second half of the 20th century, indigenous Fijians and Indo-Fijians have been roughly equal in size. However, the Indo-Fijian population has been in rapid decline since the late 1980s, in large part due to emigration following from the 1987 and 2000 coups. According to the latest statistics, indigenous Fijians account for 54.8 percent of the total population; Indo-Fijians 37.4 percent and "others" 7.8 percent (Fiji Islands Bureau of Statistics 2006).

[10] Fiji's current system of parliamentary representation under the 1997 Constitution provides for 71 seats in the House of Representatives, of which 23 are allocated to indigenous Fijians, 19 for Indo-Fijians, 1 for Rotumans, 3 for General Electors

been the dominant discourse through which Fiji's conflicts have manifested, the root causes of Fiji's woes are far more complex and deeply rooted in its historical legacy of societal segregation,[11] its indigenous institutions, and the country's persistent struggles with democratization.

Fiji faced enormous challenges after the 2000 coup, which had the effect of overthrowing democracy, inflicting pain and loss on many families, disintegrating the country into lawlessness, escalating ethnic tensions, and bringing the country's economy to its knees. The country was at the crossroads, with many daunting questions unresolved. Will democracy and the rule of law return after yet another violent overthrow of government? Will indigenous Fijian political supremacy, already guaranteed in the country's laws, be further expanded to deny other groups' rightful participation in society? How will criminal accountability be delivered to the perpetrators of violence? How can Fiji's communities, affected by violence, outbreak of racial fervor and lawlessness, heal the wounds of the past and together build a shared future?

In the months after the 2000 coup, Fiji's politicians, religious leaders, ethnic community leaders and civil society all called for a process of national reconciliation. This consensus on the need for reconciliation resonates with growing international recognition of reconciliation and transitional justice processes as central tasks in post-conflict societies seeking to address the legacy of a violent past and build a just and peaceful future. Despite the abundance of international experiences, Fiji would need to find its own path to reconciliation with its unique historical, political and societal circumstances.

The following sections will analyze the process of reconciliation undertaken in Fiji after the 2000 coup, with attention on reconciliation as

(representatives from other ethnic groups), and 25 "Open Seats" for candidates irrespective of ethnicity. The Senate consists of 32 members, of which 14 are appointed by the Great Council of Chiefs, 9 by the Prime Minister, 8 by the Leader of the Opposition and 1 by the Council of Rotuma.

[11] Out of both administrative expediency and a desire to preserve indigenous Fijians' traditional way of life, colonial rulers isolated the indigenous communities from other groups and locked them into a subsistence economy under rigid traditional institutional structures. The Indo-Fijian community, having endured a difficult life in the indenture era, was able to develop into relative prosperity in post-indenture decades through acquiring better education and achieving success in business and sugarcane farming on leased indigenous land. The societal segregation of the two main ethnic groups, while safeguarding against the erosion of indigenous culture and customs, denied meaningful interaction between the indigenous Fijian and Indo-Fijian communities throughout the colonial era (e.g. Lal 2002).

promoted by the Qarase-led SDL Coalition Government which presided over Fiji from July 2000 until December 2006 when it was deposed by a military coup. The analysis will place emphasis on "political reconciliation"[12] and "civic trust"[13] processes; of political and wider societal processes that engender equity and trust among groups in conflict based on justice, rule of law and democratic principles. The focus on political and wider societal processes in this chapter does not seek to diminish the valuable contribution towards healing and restoration of relationships undertaken at community and interpersonal levels, including those based on traditional and religious mechanisms. Moreover, considering reconciliation is still very much an evolving field, both in theory and practice, and the fact that its constituent tasks are heavily dependent on each society's unique historical and political contexts, the following analysis seeks to avoid evaluating Fiji's path from a standardized, externally imposed and overtly scholastic model. Rather, greater practical contribution can be made to this field of work by allowing Fiji's unique circumstances to inform and complement our existing—but perhaps yet inadequate—understanding of the challenging task of building lasting peace in a post-conflict society.

Political Reconciliation in Post-Coup Fiji: The SDL Coalition Years

The High Court's decision in the Chandrika Prasad case[14] in March 2001 which declared the illegality of the military's abrogation of the 1997 Constitution, and consequently the illegality of the Qarase-led Interim Government, led to the country's first post-coup election in September 2001. With the shadow of the coup looming large over the election campaign, Qarase's indigenous-dominated SDL party won power on a

---

[12] Political reconciliation refers to national reconciliation processes that involve the creation and respect of new political and societal structures based on justice, rule of law and democratic principles (e.g. Bloomfield 2006).

[13] The International Center for Transitional Justice Reconciliation (ICTJ) also views reconciliation as something that occurs in the civic or political sphere, rather than at the level of individuals. It distinguishes legitimate reconciliation from efforts to use reconciliation as a substitute for justice. This view treats reconciliation as more than just a state of mind, but as a process to engender trust among groups and between groups and their institutions based on principles of justice and equality, and achieved by tasks such as institutional reform, truth-telling, reparations and criminal accountability (ICTJ 2006).

[14] Republic of Fiji Islands v Prasad [2001] FJCA 2 (March 1, 2001).

wave of indigenous nationalism, and formed a coalition government with a party[15] of indigenous ethnonationalists that not only supported the coup, but fielded candidates who were subsequently convicted for their involvement. With the erosion of law and order and the country's communities more polarized than ever, the task of national reconciliation fell to a government delivered to power on the premise of further entrenching indigenous Fijian interests.

Despite assuming power on an ethnonationalist agenda, Qarase was keen to demonstrate to the country's multiethnic communities and to the international community that his government was committed to restoring democratic rule and promoting justice and reconciliation. Declaring reconciliation as a national priority "indispensable to the healing of Fiji" (Qarase 2000), Qarase created a Ministry of National Reconciliation and Unity in September 2000, tasked not only to promote harmony between Fiji's ethnic groups, but also to promote unity within the indigenous Fijian community (Fiji 2001).[16] The creation of the Ministry was accompanied by the formation of a National Council of Reconciliation, an advisory body to the government on reconciliation matters.

The politicization of reconciliation

Qarase's stated commitment to reconciliation was proclaimed alongside pledges to further indigenous Fijian interests through a series of policies, including affirmative action programs aimed to benefit only indigenous Fijians;[17] amendment of land tenancy legislation to bring more benefit to indigenous land owners; and a review of the 1997 Constitution with the aim of ensuring that only an indigenous Fijian can hold the

---

[15] Conservative Alliance Matanitu Vanua (CAMV), which merged with SDL ahead of the 2006 General Elections.

[16] The Ministry of Reconciliation's Strategic Plan 2001-2003 describes the aims of the Ministry as "promoting racial harmony and social cohesion through social, cultural, educational, sports and other activities and projects at the neighborhood, community, district, divisional and national level," and "promoting greater unity within the indigenous Fijian community through various program and activities at the village, *tikina*, provincial and national levels."

[17] The affirmative action policies based on ethnicity pursued by the Qarase government are found in the Social Justice Act 2001, Blueprint for the Protection of Fijian & Rotuman Rights and Interests, and the Advancement of Their Development (Fiji 2000) and 50/50 by Year 2020: 20-Year Development Plan (2001-2020) for the Enhancement of Participation of Indigenous Fijians and Rotumans in the Socio-Economic Development of Fiji (Fiji 2002). These programs were mainly based on providing business incentives for indigenous Fijians.

position of the Prime Minister (Robertson and Sutherland 2002).[18] Although drawing condemnation both domestically and abroad, Qarase's policies to further indigenous Fijian interests crucially won support from indigenous nationalist constituencies, as well as the Great Council of Chiefs, the body established during the colonial era to safeguard indigenous Fijian interests.[19] Fiji's reconciliation process was off to a controversial start.

Shortly after its creation, the Ministry of Reconciliation undertook nationwide consultations seeking to understand the root causes of the 2000 coup. In planning its strategy, it considered international experiences by sending a team of representatives to South Africa, a country undergoing a high-profile reconciliation process, and Malaysia, a country with comparable ethnic dynamics. Staff from the Ministry and the National Council also traveled to rural communities that were affected by the coup, in an attempt to facilitate community level reconciliation between those who suffered from racially-motivated violence and their perpetrators.[20]

Despite some useful works in exploring the root causes of the 2000 coup and generating goodwill among Fiji's communities, the Ministry's programs were primarily focused on holding workshops and community consultation fora, as well as sponsorship of ethnic, religious, cultural and sporting events. Both the Ministry and the National Council generally steered clear of some of the more sensitive issues such as racial discrimination and religious intolerance, largely due to the fact that the source of these inflammatory acts were often attributed to government policy and hate speeches from its own parliamentarians and Ministers.[21]

---

[18] Under the 1997 Constitution, the President and Deputy President positions are already effectively reserved for indigenous Fijians, as they are appointed by the Great Council of Chiefs.

[19] The Great Council of Chiefs is an advisory body established during the colonial era consisting of the nation's indigenous chiefs from Fiji's fourteen provinces.

[20] For example, Ministry staff visited farms owned by Indo-Fijians that had been subject to torching, looting, vandalism, and in some cases, physical assault to the farmer and their family. The visits were an attempt to bring together the farmers and those who engaged in the violent acts, most of whom were indigenous Fijian youths from nearby villages.

[21] Racially provocative remarks were frequently uttered by SDL Coalition parliamentarians under parliamentary privilege unrestrained by Qarase. For example, former Minister for Social Welfare and Poverty Alleviation Asenaca Caucau said that indigenous Fijians must "watch over fellow Indo-Fijians because they are like weeds. They tend to push to grab and take over the land and the nation" (Parliament of Fiji Hansard, House of Representatives, July 28, 2002). Senator Adi Litia Cakobau called for a ban of the term 'Indo-Fijian', the usage of

The Ministry's work was evidently restricted by its set-up as a government department, and having Qarase as the Minister for Reconciliation for the most part of its existence. Due to its lack of institutional independence, scarcity of resources and absence of any statutory authority, the scope and effectiveness of the Ministry's work was severely constrained. The National Council also struggled due to limitations of the same kind. Although its membership included some distinguished figures from Fiji's diverse communities, its legitimacy suffered through the fact that its 15-person membership was handpicked by the Prime Minister and devoid of wider consultation.

The Qarase Government's approach to reconciliation was in large part shaped by what it perceived as the root cause of Fiji's problem, that being indigenous Fijians' fears of Indo-Fijian domination. Notwithstanding the overly simplistic nature of this assertion, by highlighting ethnic differences and competing interests, the government contributed little to promoting multiethnic harmony and shared values, and instead further reinforced existing ethnic attachments. The government also sought political gains through highly ambiguous interpretations of "reconciliation" and "unity" manifested through activities sponsored by the Ministry of Reconciliation. A major stated aim of the Ministry was to promote "unity" among indigenous Fijians under the erroneous assertion that national reconciliation can only be achieved if reconciliation happens first among indigenous Fijians (ECREA 2001). Political self-interest evidently drove the government's motives for reconciliation, for Qarase knew well that the surest way to retain political ascendancy was to rally all indigenous Fijians under one political banner. The devotion of a significant part of the reconciliation budget to promote indigenous Fijian solidarity also served to exclude the Indo-Fijian community, the primary victims of the 2000 coup, from being meaningfully involved in the reconciliation process.

The use and abuse of religion

Religious affiliation in Fiji is strongly divided along ethnic lines—almost all indigenous Fijians are Christians, with the vast majority of

---

which was described by her as a "subtle and devious means of psychological domination being systematically employed by social engineers of Indian origin to usurp the name 'Fijian'" (Parliament of Fiji Hansard, Senate, July 2, 2004). Senator Mitieli Bulanauca called for a Christian state and for the sacking of judges of Indian and European ethnicity because they "hate indigenous Fijians and they should be sacked and sent out of the country" (RNZI, December 16, 2002).

Indo-Fijians being either Hindus or Muslims.[22] Religious prejudice has often been employed by indigenous nationalists seeking to exploit the ethno-religious divide through using Christianity as a unifying force and justification for indigenous political supremacy (e.g. Srebrnik 2002, Ratuva 2002). The Methodist Church, which commands the respect of the majority of indigenous Fijians, has in particular been closely linked with indigenous nationalism, with many of its leaders lending support to the 1987 and 2000 coups. Such public rhetoric was a significant factor in triggering racially-motivated attacks on Hindu temples. The Qarase Government's habitually muted response to incidents of religious sacrilege was striking and drew heated criticism from the Indo-Fijian and wider communities.

In promoting reconciliation, the SDL Coalition Government sought to draw on the religious reverence of Fiji Islanders by designating 2004 as the "National Year of Prayer". The majority of events organized under this theme contained an overtly evangelical Christian fervor, focusing on strengthening individuals' reverence of God.[23] Significant state resources were diverted to events such as the National Day of Prayer and Fasting, which comprised of separate prayer sessions for Fiji's different religious groups. Many of the events under National Year of Prayer were ill-conceived and evidently not designed to encourage inter-religious dialogue and understanding. Rather, they served to reinforce existing religious identities. Civil society groups advocating cross-religious understanding, such as Interfaith Search Fiji and ECREA,[24] refused to support the tokenism of such events.

The Qarase Government's employment of overtly Christian concepts of reconciliation failed to be effective on two grounds. First, given that the vast majority of the Indo-Fijian population subscribe to non-Christian faiths, and the fact that indigenous nationalists have used Christianity to justify the racist motive of the 1987 and 2000 coups, an overtly Christian approach to reconciliation only served to alienate the Indo-Fijian

---

[22] More than 99 percent of indigenous Fijians are subscribed to one of the Christian denominations, with Methodists being the dominant group (67 percent) followed by Catholics (13 percent) and other denominations. The majority of Indo-Fijians are Hindus (78 percent), with a sizeable Muslim minority (16 percent) and a small percentage of Christians (6 percent) (Fiji Islands Bureau of Statistics 2006).

[23] For example, an advertisement by the Ministry of Reconciliation on the National Day of Prayer and Fasting described that prayer and fasting can become a catalyst for reconciliation. It also stated that people of Fiji should "seek God's guidance in order to achieve unity in the Spirit" (Daily Post, July 6, 2004).

[24] Ecumenical Centre for Research, Advocacy and Education (Suva, Fiji).

community. Moreover, the government's focus on interpersonal reconciliation processes derived from Christian concepts was misplaced and created confusion among the public. An example of the confusion between interpersonal and national processes of reconciliation is evident in the Ministry of Reconciliation's public pamphlet, which curiously claimed that reconciliation is achieved when "one does not feel he has done any wrong" (Ministry of Reconciliation 2002). The Ministry's promotion of reconciliation was underpinned by concepts such as confession, repentance and forgiveness. Although these interpersonal processes could be effective in certain situations, they were inadequate in the context of the wider societal, political and judicial processes required at the national level.

The reconciliation process promoted by the Qarase Government was widely regarded as lacking legitimacy, ill-conceived and heavily politicized. It generated confusion,[25] suspicion and distrust among Fiji's communities, and was routinely criticized by Fiji's political leaders, civil society, and religious leaders. The politicization of reconciliation would serve as a decisive obstacle to the country's elusive search for truth and justice.

Justice Denied: Perpetuating Impunity, Indignity and Inequality

For a society that has experienced episodes of violent conflict, political disruption and societal inequality, the attainment of justice is undoubtedly the most central task in any process that seeks to address the legacy of the past and lay foundations for peaceful coexistence. International experience demonstrates that justice and reconciliation are twin notions in post-conflict contexts: without attaining justice, reconciliation is incomplete, hollow and unsustainable (IDEA 2003). The political and societal context of Fiji after the 2000 coup demanded justice to be addressed in a multidimensional way, including: bringing to account those who committed unlawful acts; providing reparation and restoring dignity of

---

[25] For instance, in 2004 the Ministry inexplicably devoted significant resources in organizing an elaborate ceremony on behalf of an indigenous clan that had cannibalized a British missionary in the late 19th century. The ceremony, promoted as the government's commitment to reconciliation, involved the indigenous clan seeking forgiveness from the Australian descendents of the deceased Reverend Thomas Baker.

victims; educating the public about the past; and engendering equitable societal participation.

In the shadows of 1987 and 2000: breaking the cycle of impunity

The 2000 coup brought untold suffering to the country. Not only was democracy again thwarted by force, widespread violence was committed against the Indo-Fijian community, including the looting and burning of property, vandalism of places of worship, and incidents of physical and sexual assault. The violence in 2000 was much more widespread than in 1987 and again triggered mass emigration of Indo-Fijians, including some of Fiji's best qualified professionals.

An assessment of the attainment of criminal accountability arising from the 2000 coup needs to be considered in light of the legacy from 1987. Following his violent takeover of Parliament, Rabuka and all his accomplices were granted blanket amnesty by Governor-General Sir Ratu Penaia Ganilau.[26] Despite plunging the country into years of social, economic and political crisis and international isolation, the conferment of immunity from prosecution to Rabuka and his accomplices gave the 1987 coup its ultimate legitimacy. This impunity to criminal justice meant that the brutality and violence of the 1987 coup would not serve as a deterrent, but an inspiration, for the would-be perpetrators of 2000.

After violence had subsided in 2000, bringing to account perpetrators of the coup and its violent aftermath was central to building confidence and trust in the communities. Like Rabuka before him, Speight and his group sought, and were duly granted, amnesty by the military during the hostage crisis. The military decree granting immunity was however subsequently annulled by Fiji's Courts in the Prasad case that upheld the validity of the 1997 Constitution. This paved the way for the prosecution and eventual conviction and incarceration of Speight and a number of his leading accomplices.

Speight and his front men were just the tip of the iceberg. The process of identifying and prosecuting those behind the 2000 coup also carried significant political implications. Numerous figures that were involved in the coup, both directly and peripherally, were now holding office as parliamentarians and ministers within Qarase's SDL Coalition Government. There was significant pressure placed upon the Qarase

[26] The Governor-General, Fiji's head of state before it became a republic, possessed reserved powers at times of emergency.

Government, both from domestic and international sources, to proactively pursue these perpetrators of violence. However, the government's political hold depended greatly on support from its extreme ethnonationalist coalition partners. Qarase's decision to appoint those under charge for coup offences as ministers, and reward those under investigation with lucrative diplomatic posts,[27] drew intense criticism from Fiji's communities. The sight of coup accomplices holding high office and shielded by the government was an insult to many, and only served to further belittle the victims' suffering.

After a string of highly publicized trials, several high profile figures were convicted of coup-related offences by Fiji's courts in 2004 and 2005. These convictions claimed a number of serving politicians, including Vice President Ratu Jope Seniloli, government ministers, and parliamentarians.[28] The convictions were hailed as a significant victory for the rule of law, and restored some public faith in the judiciary after its tainted reputation from the 2000 hostage crisis.[29] Qarase's coalition team, suffering from the embarrassment of conviction of its parliamentarians and ardent supporters, proceeded to spuriously employ arbitrary powers of the Attorney-General to secure the early release of convicted politicians in acts that were regarded by Fiji's legal fraternity as a blatant interference in the justice system (RNZI April 15, 2005). The release of Seniloli was facilitated after only three months into his four-year sentence on health grounds. Similarly, several former government ministers were released to serve their terms extramurally shortly after their incarceration.[30] The government's far-reaching acts to protect convicted politicians drew public outcry and

[27] For example, the Police Commissioner during the 2000 coup, Isikia Savua, was widely believed to be implicated in the coup. He was appointed by Qarase to be Fiji's Ambassador to the United Nations.

[28] The serving politicians convicted between 2004 and 2005 for coup-related offences include: Ratu Jope Seniloli (Vice President), Ratu Rakuita Vakalalabure (Deputy Speaker, House of Representatives), Ratu Inoke Takiveikata (Senator), Apisai Tora (Senator), Ratu Naiqama Lalabalavu (Minister for Lands and Natural Resources) and Ratu Josefa Dimuri (Senator).

[29] The independence of the judiciary was called into question when, during the height of the hostage crisis in the 2000 coup, three members of Fiji's High Court reportedly advised President Ratu Mara to abrogate the Constitution, as requested by the Fiji Military. Ratu Mara opposed such measures and was reportedly pressured into resignation by Bainimarama (Daily Post July 25, 2002).

[30] For example, former Lands Minister Ratu Naiqama Lalabalavu and Senator Josefa Dimuri were released eleven days into their eight-month sentences. Former Deputy Speaker of the House of Representatives Ratu Rakuita Vakalalabure was released two years into his six-year sentence.

furious protest from opposition parties and non-government organizations (NGOs), and further antagonized the already inimical relationship between itself and the military.[31]

Despite government interference, conviction of some of the players of the accomplices of the 2000 coup represented a significant step forward from 1987 in the attainment of criminal accountability. The message was unmistakable: that the vicious cycle of impunity that started in 1987 must end, and that the removal of an elected government by force, for whatever political end, has no place in Fiji's democratic future. Significantly, the conviction of coup perpetrators also facilitated an important step towards national reconciliation through fulfilling an obligation to the coup's victims and restoring their faith in the country's institutions.

Aside from the conviction of some high-profile figures, investigations and prosecutions stemming from the 2000 coup have proceeded at a painstakingly slow pace due to an overburdened criminal justice system.[32] This lack of progress, coupled with the SDL Coalition Government's attempts to protect coup accomplices, and further set back by the latest coup which has seen the military erode the independence of the police force, means that justice and criminal accountability for past coup perpetrators may remain elusive for the foreseeable future.

Amnesty, Forgiveness and the Reconciliation Bill

Throughout its time in office, the SDL Coalition Government sought to place particular emphasis on "forgiveness" in its promotion of reconciliation, with Qarase stressing that "one needed to forgive unconditionally before attempting reconciliation" (Qarase 2000). The call for forgiveness was put forward as a Christian-inspired element of reconciliation, but the government's underlying motivation to protect coup perpetrators was conspicuous. Qarase's announcement of 2005 as the "National Year of Forgiveness" was again met with suspicion, as it coincided with the conviction of government parliamentarians and the

---

[31] Bainimarama's motivation to see justice done to 2000 coup perpetrators has been in part due to his personal near-escape from a mutiny executed by nationalist soldiers in November 2000, which was eventually put down brutally resulting in the death of five rebel and three loyalist soldiers.

[32] As of January 2006, over 2000 people had been processed by the police for coup-related offences, among which 782 were charged and convicted for a total of 28 offences. Former Police Commissioner Andrew Hughes attributed the slow pace of investigations to the sheer volume of cases and the lack of willingness of witnesses to cooperate in divulging information (Fiji Police January 5, 2006).

state's interference in gaining their early release. The focus on forgiveness also sought to place the onus of reconciliation on the Indo-Fijian community, while deflecting attention from government policies that undermined reconciliation and the attainment of justice. The events organized during the National Year of Forgiveness were boycotted and dismissed as hollow and tokenistic by the victims of the 2000 coup, including Chaudhry's Fiji Labour Party (FLP), as well as the military and large sections of the civil society.[33]

The introduction of the Promotion of Reconciliation, Tolerance and Unity Bill (Reconciliation Bill) in May 2005 was no doubt the government's most controversial initiative. The Bill proposed the creation of a commission to conduct hearings into breaches of human rights committed in 2000 and to grant reparation to victims. The main controversy related to a clause that allowed the commission to grant amnesty to those who committed crimes during the 2000 coup under a "political motivation", as opposed to deliberate criminal intent. The amnesty provision drew strong opposition from many sections of the society, including FLP, the Fiji Law Society (FLS), and the Fiji Human Rights Commission (FHRC). Both FHRC and the FLS warned that the Bill contained numerous breaches of the Constitution, in particular its undermining of the role of the judiciary (FHRC 2005, FLS 2005). Fiji's NGO Coalition on Human Rights organized street rallies in protest of the Bill, claiming it a blatant attempt by the government to short-cut the justice process in providing protection for those who committed coup offences (CCF 2005). The Bill also drew vociferous condemnation from Bainimarama, with the military threatening to remove the government if it was not withdrawn.[34]

---

[33] One of the proposed events included a traditional indigenous apology offered by Ratu Naiqama Lalabalavu (then Minister for Lands and Natural Resources) to Mahendra Chaudhry and all parliamentarians taken hostage in May 2000. The motive and timing of the apology was however considered highly opportunistic as Lalabalavu was under charge for a coup-related offence, for which he was subsequently convicted. Chaudhry and FLP members boycotted the event, considering the offer to be insincere. The event was also strongly opposed by the military. Lalabalavu nevertheless went ahead and presented a traditional indigenous *matanigasau* apology to President Ratu Josefa Iloilo in a national ceremony.

[34] The Fiji Military, in its submission to the Parliamentary Sector Standing Committee on Justice, Law and Order, said that "The Republic of Fiji Military Forces must stop the bill from passing or get rid of the government if it is passed … We can recover without this government but we cannot recover from this bill." (Pacific Magazine July 12, 2005). Bainimarama repeated the threat to remove the

The Reconciliation Bill was indeed a deeply flawed, regressive and politically motivated proposal. The granting of amnesty to offenders would equate to legitimation of treasonous and violent criminal acts, and serve to encourage, rather than deter, future acts that seek to bring about political change through illegal and violent means. The Indo-Fijian community regarded the amnesty proposal a further insult to the victims of 2000, who were yet to receive any official recognition for their hurt and suffering (FLP 2005, Fijilive June 13, 2005).[35] Furthermore, there was no requirement for the hearings of the commission to be conducted in public. This would not only shield its works from public scrutiny, but also deny a critical opportunity for the public to learn about the truth of the 2000 coup through testimonies of victims and offenders.

Under intense pressure from the public, and recognizing its negative political impact, the government withdrew the Reconciliation Bill before the 2006 election. For an initiative that purported to promote reconciliation, the Bill only succeeded in generating outrage and heightening societal tension.

The absence of truth, reparation and healing

The primary attainment of justice since the 2000 coup has been through legal processes of criminal prosecutions. This type of "retributive justice" based on punishment of criminals has been important in individualizing guilt and providing the deterrence effect critical to a country with a history of coups. However, criminal prosecutions alone have not brought healing or a complete sense of justice for victims. In addition to the Indo-Fijian community, which bore the brunt of post-coup violence, the destructive effects of the 2000 coup inflicted hurt and loss to all communities due to its overthrow of the country's democratic institutions, the general erosion of law and order, and the associated economic downturn which claimed thousands of jobs.

There were repeated calls for the SDL Coalition Government to accept responsibility in providing reparation and healing for victims through compensation and restorative justice mechanisms. However, evidently

---

government some months later, stating that "If they lack the moral strength and the courage to continue the good fight, the military is willing to return and complete for this nation the responsibilities we gave this government in 2000 and 2001." (Fiji Times January 9, 2006).

[35] There was no requirement for those seeking amnesty to apologize or demonstrate remorse for their actions. Furthermore, amnesty was to be granted by commissioners, regardless whether forgiveness had been conferred by victims.

sympathetic to the coup's objectives, the government consistently refused to consider compensation until its inclusion in the ill-conceived Reconciliation Bill alongside the controversial amnesty provisions. The government was also reluctant to even recognize the coup's illegality, with Qarase often defending the coup as an act of indigenous Fijians "answering the call of the *vanua*" (e.g. Fiji 2005).[36] The lack of genuine state recognition of the pain and injustice inflicted by the violence of 2000 was a major obstacle to reconciliation as it was seen to trivialize the victims' suffering.

Until the introduction of the Reconciliation Bill, the government had largely rejected calls for the establishment of a public inquiry to uncover the facts from 2000 coup: who were involved, what were the motivations, and how were the acts carried out. The process of truth-seeking has been a common feature in reconciliation processes internationally, having the benefit of establishing an authoritative record about the past and providing a forum for victims to tell their stories. The idea of a public inquiry was supported by Fiji's former Police Commissioner Andrew Hughes, who recognized that the criminal system alone was inadequate to deal with the scale of violations that occurred during the coup and could never reveal the whole truth (Fiji Times August 25, 2006). Whereas criminal trials seek individual guilt, a truth-telling forum has the effect of establishing historical justice and recognizing collective political and moral responsibility.

The lack of public account of the 2000 coup follows the amnesia that still blankets the 1987 coup as a result of the amnesty given to Rabuka and his accomplices. Rabuka and Speight are widely believed to be merely the front men of the real coup plotters behind the scenes. However, the identities of the so-called "shadowy figures", believed to comprise of failed politicians, businessmen and those who stood to lose out under the newly elected governments (e.g. Lal 2006, Robertson and Sutherland 2002), have never been fully revealed. The governments following the 1987 and 2000 coups have refused to engage in truth-seeking due to the fact that their very own ascendency to political power was made possible through the coups. Fiji's communities have continuously been denied an opportunity to learn from the country's past in order to put an end to its recurring crises.

The military, which had been fiercely outspoken against the government's support of coup offenders, launched its own "Justice and

[36] The *vanua* refers to the indigenous Fijians' connection with the land and their social and cultural identity, symbolized by chiefly rule. The defense of the *vanua* has been employed as a justification for the 1987 and 2000 coups.

Truth Campaign" prior to the May 2006 election to educate the public about the illegality of the acts of 2000. Despite the purported righteousness of its objectives, the military's growing involvement in the political arena would constitute a volatile addition to the societal tension that already pervaded post-coup Fiji.

Racial discrimination and inequality

A critical element in post-conflict peacebuilding lies in attaining socioeconomic and political justice through engendering fair and equitable participation for all groups. The failure to commit to a just societal structure risks breeding further discontent and undermining the broader reconciliation process. A major source of disaffection among indigenous Fijians relates to the fact that, despite owning 90 percent of land, indigenous Fijians as a group are the poorest in the country. Indigenous poverty and perceptions of Indo-Fijian wealth have often been employed as justification for maintaining indigenous political supremacy, despite the fact that indigenous leaders, who have dominated the country's political leadership since independence, have largely failed to improve the economic wellbeing of their own people.

Qarase fared no better in this respect with his controversial affirmative action program, which included a series of measures accessible to indigenous Fijians only.[37] Heavily underpinned by providing business opportunities through grants and government contracts, the affirmative action program brought benefits largely to the well-connected indigenous urban elite, rather than the most disadvantaged indigenous Fijians in peri-urban and rural areas (Reddy et al 2001, Robertson and Sutherland 2002). One core problem of the affirmative action program lay in its simplistic connection between poverty and ethnicity and its implication that all indigenous Fijians are disadvantaged. Statistics indicate that poverty exists in all ethnic communities, with some of the poorest population being Indo-Fijians. Furthermore, economic inequality within each ethnic group has been found to be far greater than between ethnic groups (UNDP 1997). The affirmative action policies, based on ethnicity rather than levels of poverty, not only failed to reach those indigenous Fijians most in need, but also denied access by disadvantaged population from other ethnic groups. The program was widely criticized both at home and abroad. The Fiji Human Rights Commission found that the program imposed "large-scale discrimination against the minority ethnic groups" and in clear breach of

---

[37] SDL Coalition Government's affirmative action policies, supra note 17.

the Bill of Rights contained in the Constitution (FHRC 2006). The United Nations Committee on the Elimination of Racial Discrimination also expressed its deep concern and recommended that the program be expanded to address poverty in all ethnic communities (UNCERD 2003).

A further manifestation of inequality relates to the disproportionate ethnic representation in key sectors of the Fijian society, largely a historical legacy of the colonial policy of political and administrative segregation. The ubiquity of Indo-Fijians in the private sector is contrasted by indigenous Fijians' historical dominance of some of the state's key institutions: the executive, the military, the civil service and the police force.[38] Indeed, many indigenous Fijians have habitually viewed the state and its apparatuses as their own. State ceremonies often begin with a Christian prayer and national events such as Fiji Day and Reconciliation Week have been primarily indigenous events (Naidu 2006). The politicization of ethnicity, the entrenchment of social economic inequality, and the legacy of ethnic segregation, have proved to be significant obstacles in the attainment of social justice and positive inter-ethnic discourse.

The denial of justice in its various forms—retributive, restorative, historical, social and economic—indicate a failure by Fiji's leaders to address the central components of reconciliation through confronting the demons of the country's past and establishing rules for the future. The reluctance of the Qarase Government to dismount from riding its wave of indigenous nationalism would ultimately contribute to its own undoing.

Reconciliation and Democratization: Toward an Uncertain Future

A major obstacle to the Qarase Government's approach to reconciliation was its lack of definition of the term itself—its meaning, its objectives, and the strategy required to achieve the desired outcomes. The heavily politicized and cosmetic nature of reconciliation promoted by the government was evidently never intended to address the challenging issues arising from Fiji's recent societal and political upheaval. Rather, reconciliation was largely employed by the government as a means to protect coup perpetrators, strengthen its own political support, and

---

[38] Indigenous Fijians have maintained numerical dominance in critical government sectors including the armed forces (99 percent), the police force (75 percent), the Permanent Secretaries (90 percent), and the civil service overall (61 percent) (Prasad et al 2001, Sriskandarajah 2003).

facilitate the attainment of coup's objectives to further entrench indigenous Fijian political supremacy.

One critical conundrum faced by Fiji since the 2000 coup relates to the fact that its quest for reconciliation has not arisen from, or been accompanied by, a process of greater peace consolidation and democratization. Fiji's context represents a stark departure from most post-conflict societies, where reconciliation has typically been an integral part of a transformative process that seeks to yield criminal accountability, just reparation, more equitable political and societal participation, and improved communal relations—in most instances following a peace settlement between groups in conflict, or after the removal of a regime that committed grave human rights abuses. In the case of Fiji, its reconciliation process was conceived and imposed by the very political group that directly benefited from the 2000 coup, an event that derailed the country's democratic path through the overthrow of its first democratically-elected government under the 1997 Constitution. Furthermore, the years following the 2000 coup, during which reconciliation has taken place, has been replete with events and political processes that have further eroded the country's democratic institutions.

Although democratic rule was purportedly restored through the 2001 General Elections won by Qarase's SDL party, its lead-up was marked by a series of controversial executive decisions that yielded profound consequences. The successful challenge of the aforementioned Prasad case, upheld by the Court of Appeals in March 2001, not only restored the 1997 Constitution and declared the Interim Government illegal, it also affirmed that the Chaudhry Government was still the country's legal government. Following the court's judgment, rather than recalling parliament and reinstating the Chaudhry Government as consistent with court declarations, President Ratu Josefa Iloilo engaged in a tenuous exercise of his reserve powers by calling for a fresh election after dissolving parliament and dismissing Chaudhry as Prime Minister. With support from the military and the GCC, Iloilo dismissed Chaudhry on the grounds that he no longer enjoyed support from his People's Coalition parliamentarians who now purportedly preferred an indigenous Fijian Prime Minister—a contention that was never verified nor tested on the floors of parliament as required by the Constitution.[39] A legal proceeding

[39] President Josefa Iloilo had evidently decided not to recall parliament and reinstate Chaudhry as the Prime Minister on the advice of the GCC and the military. He proceeded to achieve this through exercising his reserve powers purportedly within the Constitutional framework. After dismissing Chaudhry as Prime Minister, Iloilo appointed Ratu Tevita Momoedonu, a minister in

challenging this prima facie unconstitutional act failed because the matters raised were considered moot after the 2001 election had already taken place.[40]

During its time in office, the SDL Coalition Government, as already detailed, engaged in acts that further eroded Fiji's democratic institutions through its racially discriminatory policies, interference in the justice system, and attempts to enact divisive legislations designed to entrench indigenous supremacy at the expense of equitable participation of other groups. The multi-party cabinet (MPC), a power-sharing requirement under Fiji's Constitution, never eventuated after the 2001 election due to a lack of genuine commitment from both SDL and FLP. A major feature of the 1997 Constitution, the MPC was designed to encourage broad political participation and bipartisan decision-making in an attempt to steer the country away from its racialized polity.[41] The collapse of MPC negotiations was as much due to the unwillingness of SDL to compromise its pro-indigenous nationalist stance as FLP's reluctance to work with the party that claimed power courtesy of the 2000 coup. Having been the victim twice removed from government at gunpoint,[42] Chaudhry's still palpable bitterness also prevented him from reaching across the political divide.[43] The two leaders' collective failure to form the MPC after the

---

Chaudhry's People's Coalition Government, as Caretaker Prime Minister. The act was designed to facilitate the dissolution of parliament through Momedonu's advice. Momoedonu provided such advice one day after his appointment, paving the way for Iloilo to call for a new election and appoint a caretaker government headed by Qarase.

[40] Yabaki v President of the Republic of the Fiji Islands [2003] FJCA 30 (February 14, 2003).

[41] Fiji's Constitution encourages power-sharing by obligating the Prime Minister to invite into his/her cabinet members from all political parties that have gained more than 10 percent of seats in the House of Representatives. The multi-party cabinet never materialized after the 1999 and 2001 elections due to the inability of Fiji's political leaders to agree on its implementation. A multi-party cabinet was formed after the 2006 elections although it was operating under immense stress prior to the military coup with Qarase threatening to expel those FLP cabinet members who were opposed to his proposed budget.

[42] Chaudhry was the Finance Minister in the Bavadra Government that was removed by Rabuka in the 1987 coup.

[43] This was despite the best efforts of both internal and external actors, including the East-West Center in Hawai'i through its "*talanoa*" initiative that brought together the Qarase and Chaudhry teams for regular conversations moderated by a third party.

2001 election follows from the precedent set in 1999, when the FLP failed to invite Rabuka's SVT[44] party into its cabinet.

Despite its imperfections and unsuitability as a long term arrangement, the multi-party cabinet provides a practical framework to initiate political reconciliation through inclusion of all major parties, hence encouraging governance through dialogue and consensus. In the absence of adequate processes of criminal justice and truth-seeking after the 1987 coup, the enactment of the 1997 Constitution is regarded by many as the country's most significant achievement in reconciliation, realized after a process of unprecedented cooperation between indigenous and Indo-Fijian political leaders. The process that led to the promulgation of the 1997 Constitution demonstrates that a process which engenders greater political inclusion, responsible governance and respect for human rights can promote reconciliation in a divided society through laying a foundation for political cooperation and greater inter-ethnic discourse. The realization of the visions of the Constitution, however, remains a challenge for Fiji's political leaders, many of whom have much to gain from the racialised zero-sum polity that has served them well at the expense of promoting multiethnic harmony and transcultural identities.

Fiji's experience demonstrates that a successful reconciliation process needs to be interconnected with, and complementary to, a process of democratization that engenders tolerance, respect for human rights, social justice, broad political participation and greater civic trust in the country's institutions. Without a commitment to democracy that regulates relationships and manages differences through just principles, structures and processes, reconciliation is likely to be hollow and unsustainable.

Confronting the country's deep-rooted issues

Given the focus on political processes in this chapter, it is necessary to recognize that despite the failings at the political level, and the limited attainment of justice through the country's institutions, the peoples of Fiji have shown their resilience by engaging in community level initiatives that seek to engender greater inter-ethnic harmony and create micro-solutions towards resolving the country's deep-rooted issues. Leading these efforts have been Fiji's active group of NGOs, religious groups, community organizations, educational institutions, and individual champions who have worked tirelessly despite adverse political

---

44 *Soqosoqo ni Vakavulewa ni Taukei.*

circumstances. Unfortunately, these efforts have not received their deserved support at the political level.

It would be unrealistic to expect that all of Fiji's political, societal and historical dilemmas could be resolved through a reconciliation process, however genuine, comprehensive or broadly defined. A reconciliation process alone would not bring an end to Fiji's cycle of coups, the causes of which are deeply rooted in the country's historical legacies and its political and societal structure. Fiji's dilemmas are far more complex than grievances between ethnic groups; they relate to broader processes of democratization and difficult questions relating to the role of its indigenous institutions. Despite the depth of its challenges, a genuine and inclusive process of reconciliation, conducted alongside a process of engendering greater democracy, equality and respect for human rights, would lay the foundation for resolving the country's deep-rooted issues through building better working relationships and establishing fairer principles for the society. A brief account of the country's deep-rooted issues follows.

Fiji's ethnic-based electoral system, although guaranteeing representation from all communities, has encouraged political parties to be formed along ethnic lines. It reinforces ethnic attachments, rewards ethnic chauvinism, and ensures that public issues are perpetually viewed and contested through ethnic lenses. A change in the electoral system, though urgently needed, would however only be part of the solution. Successive indigenous leaders have referred to democracy as a "foreign flower"; a western concept unsuitable to indigenous aspirations. However, as Robertson and Sutherland (2002) argue, indigenous Fijians, like other groups, rely on democratic institutions to bring about the transparency, accountability, and equitable participation needed for their social and economic development. Indigenous political supremacy, aside from violating universal principles of human rights and equality, would fail to address indigenous aspirations as it only encourages bad governance and corruption through the removal of democratic mechanisms that hold to account a government's performance.

A further dilemma relates to Fiji's indigenous institutions, such as the Great Council of Chiefs, the Provincial Councils and the Native Land Trust Board. These quasi-traditional institutions, which have functioned as a parallel system of governance alongside the country's Westminster political system, were constructs from the colonial era that sought to protect indigenous interests in an ethnically segregated society under British rule. They have also been the very institutions that have been ignominiously involved in the indigenous ethno-nationalism during the country's recent crises. Reforming indigenous Fijian governance has been a highly emotive and sensitive issue that often results in politicization along ethnic lines, hence stifling dispassionate debate on an issue critical to the country's future. In a post-colonial, globalized and multicultural society where indigenous Fijians are no longer threatened as the majority group, it is critical that indigenous institutions are capable of bringing genuine benefits to indigenous Fijians, while playing a positive role in the overall national development.

Fiji's greatest dilemma of all, however, relates to the role of its military, an institution that became politicized with the 1987 coup. With an almost exclusively indigenous Fijian make-up, the military was the vehicle through which indigenous ethnonationalism was advanced in 1987. It has since demonstrated its willingness to force its will on Fiji's political life, playing a central role in the events of 2000 and now executing the country's fourth overthrow of government in nineteen years. How can it be expected to serve its rightful role in a democratic society? For the moment, it appears that Fiji's future rests not with the will of its peoples or its political leaders, but with the guns of the military.

A "democratic" coup? The military takeover of December 2006

The military coup of December 5, 2006 that overthrew the Qarase Government materialized after several years of tension between the government and the military, escalating to repeated threats by Bainimarama to remove the government in the months leading up to its eventual execution. This latest coup, the aftermath of which is still unfolding as this chapter is finalized, may at first glance confound casual observers. The absence of an overt racial motive immediately sets it apart from previous coups. Furthermore, it was Bainimarama who, bowing to pressure from indigenous ethno-nationalists during the 2000 crisis, abrogated the 1997 Constitution and installed Qarase to head the Interim Government.

Bainimarama's stated reasons for waging what he termed the "Clean Up Campaign" are centered on a fervent moral conviction: that for the good of the country, he was left with no choice but to intervene and put an end to the policies of the Qarase Government which he claimed were corrupt and racist. For a man who has long portrayed himself as the savior who rescued the country from near-total destruction in 2000, Bainimarama felt betrayed by the government's continual protection of coup perpetrators. His determination in this respect is also deeply personal, having nearly lost his life in November 2000 in an army mutiny carried out by rebel soldiers who supported Speight's coup. Bainimarama sought to morally justify his takeover on the government's undemocratic practices: its racially discriminatory policies and its continuing incitement of ethnic tensions; its proposed bills relating to land and coastal waters that would purportedly fan indigenous nationalism and destroy the tourism industry;[45] and its alleged engagement in corruption, including in the 2006 elections, and of ministers and civil servants (RFMF Press Release January 4, 2007).

Bainimarama's stated motivations portray a man on a mission to bring justice, equality and good governance to a country ravaged by successive coups. His message is clear: that a coup was inevitable for the greater good of the country. Could this utterly undemocratic act actually yield a democratic outcome? Bainimarama's rationale, however, is fatally flawed. The latest coup further sets back Fiji's struggles to overcome its "culture of coups"; to manage political difference through peaceful means within the confines of the country's democratic and constitutional framework. Early developments bring little cause for optimism that the latest coup would bring about the greater democracy and justice promised by Bainimarama. In an attempt to legitimize his takeover, Bainimarama "returned" executive authority to President Iloilo on January 4, 2007. On the following day, the President duly appointed the Military Commander as Interim Prime Minister, and proceeded to confirm the widespread speculation that he supported the military takeover. Bainimarama has since further tightened his grip on power by dismissing top level civil servants and government-appointed statutory board members, suspending the Chief Justice of the High Court, suspending the Great Council of Chiefs, placing the country under a state of emergency, and limiting freedom of expression by rounding up civil society activists who publicly voice their opposition to the coup.

Most critically, the latest coup has once again entrenched Fiji's cycle of violence and impunity. Under Bainimarama's tutelage, Iloilo proceeded to grant full prosecutorial immunity to the military and all associated with the December 2006 coup.[46] Bainimarama sees no irony in the fact that one of his primary reasons for ousting the Qarase Government was its

---

[45] The Qoliqoli Bill and the Indigenous Claims Tribunal Bill.

[46] In his statement of January 5, 2007, Iloilo conferred a list of mandates for the Interim Government headed by Bainimarama, including facilitation of all legal protection and immunity to the Military Commander, officers and all members of the Fiji Military (Fiji Times January 5, 2007).

protection of 2000 coup perpetrators. The failure to comprehensively address criminal accountability from 1987 and 2000 continues to cast a long shadow over the country's future. The seeking and granting of amnesty has become a customary feature in the planning, execution, resolution and legitimation of coups, a strategy Bainimarama has gleefully adopted from Rabuka and Speight. Out of the three, Speight, the only coup maker who failed to muster full backing from the military, is also the only one who has been subjected to criminal accountability.

For all the harm the latest coup has inflicted on Fiji's political future, fortunately it has not brought about the overt racism and communal violence that followed the 1987 and 2000 coups. Those opposed to the military takeover have sullenly acquiesced to life under military rule, while many others regard the coup as a regrettable but necessary outcome. One perplexing phenomenon has been the fact that the latest coup has sharply polarized pro-democratic advocates in the country, the very group that had been steadfastly united in their opposition to the 1987 and 2000 coups. Many belonging to this group, including political parties and civil society organizations, have either voiced their support for the military takeover or have been conspicuously muted in their opposition. The Fiji Labour Party and the National Alliance Party wasted no time in joining Bainimarama's Interim Government, raising suspicions that they supported the military takeover all along. The Fiji Human Rights Commission, led by its Director Shaista Shameem, has vehemently defended the military coup, arguing that there were few options given the grave extent to which the Qarase Government undermined the country's enjoyment of democracy and human rights (FHRC 2007a). Shameem's publication of elaborate legal justifications for the coup has been heavily criticized and dismissed by many of Fiji's constitutional and human rights lawyers (e.g. FHRC 2007b), and has compromised the independence of the Commission[47] while emboldening the Bainimarama-led regime. Even

[47] FHRC's membership of the International Coordination Committee of National Institutions for the Promotion and Protection of Human Rights (ICC) was suspended in March 2007 after it was found to be in non-compliance with the Paris Principles, the international minimum standards required by a national human rights institution to effectively fulfill its role (APF 2007). FHRC claims that it withdrew its ICC membership before the suspension and has referred the matter to the UN Ombudsman (Shameem pers. com., November 18, 2007). In tandem with the actions of the ICC, the Asia Pacific Forum of National Human Rights Institutions (APF) initiated a review of FHRC in March 2007. FHRC withdrew its membership from APF in April 2007, citing that APF was biased in its assessment of FHRC (Shameem pers. com., November 18, 2007). FHRC currently has no

if the latest coup could ever be morally justified for its righteous purpose, it serves to further entrench Fiji's frightening norm of overthrowing elected governments as a legitimate means of resolving political difference.

Given the way reconciliation has been thoroughly abused, misused and politicized by Fiji's political leaders since the 2000 coup, the term "reconciliation" no longer yields meaningful outcomes in the political sphere, and arguably should be abandoned altogether for the foreseeable future. The pursuit of justice, truth, reparation, criminal accountability and institutional reforms arising from Fiji's conflicts can no longer be helpfully described or advanced in terms of reconciliation. The latest military coup, once again usurping Fiji's fragile democracy, has further eliminated reconciliation from the public discourse—symbolized by the Bainimarama's decision to disband the Ministry of National Reconciliation and Unity (Fiji Times March 22, 2007).[48]

Despite the latest crisis, and uncertainty over when the country will return to democratic rule, many Fiji Islanders remain cautiously optimistic about their future. Although most regard the military takeover as a regrettable outcome, Bainimarama's stated objectives have resonated widely, with many believing that the coup may actually present an opportunity to bring about the necessary political and institutional reforms that would have otherwise been unlikely under Fiji's contemporary leaders and racialised polity. Furthermore, progress in restoring constitutionalism and establishing criminal accountability since 2000—however inadequate and despite being derailed by the latest coup—indicate the existence of a generally robust and resilient justice system that has survived successive coups and attempts at its politicization. The conviction of some of the 2000 coup perpetrators gives hope that Fiji is at least slowly on the path towards breaking the cycle of impunity and establishing rules for the future. Intense diplomatic efforts and pressure by Fiji's Pacific neighbors have also produced some desirable outcomes, evidenced by Bainimarama pledge to hold national elections by 2009 (Fiji 2007).

Fiji was once hailed "the way the world should be" because of its natural beauty and multiethnic peaceful coexistence. Despite conflicts and ethnic mobilizations at the political level, and outbreaks of racial violence

---

speaking rights at the UN Human Rights Council due to its non-compliance with the Paris Principles.

[48] At the time of publication, there were reports that the Ministry of Reconciliation may be re-established to provide support to the proposed People's Charter for Change and Progress (Fiji Times November 22, 2007).

following the 1987 and 2000 coups, inter-ethnic relations in the country have generally remained amicable at the grassroots. Fiji's communities will need to draw on all their resilience to pull the country out of its recurring crises, as they grapple with the true meaning and purpose of reconciliation, justice and democracy.

Conclusion

In the wake of Fiji's *coup d'état* of 2000, which unleashed an unprecedented level of violence and destruction to the country, the peoples of Fiji demanded a process of national reconciliation to heal the wounds of the past and build a more peaceful future. Fiji's troubled path to reconciliation has been marked by its failure to address issues of justice that lie at the heart of reconciliation: bringing to account perpetrators of violence, providing just reparation for victims, ensuring fair and equitable social and economic participation, and creating an opportunity for the country's communities to learn from its recent history of violence.

The reconciliation process promoted by Laisenia Qarase's SDL Coalition Government was heavily politicized and cosmetic. It was conducted absent of clear goals and outcomes, and devoid of widespread and meaningful participation from Fiji's communities. Furthermore, with its unwavering support of the objectives of the coup and its protection of coup perpetrators, the government's interference in the justice system undermined the gains made through the conviction of several high-profile political figures.

Fiji's reconciliation process was also doomed because it was not advanced alongside a process that promoted greater peace and democratization. The military takeover of December 2006, which will only further set back Fiji's struggles with democratic governance and the rule of law, is directly related to the country's failure to deal with issues of justice and criminal accountability from its recent past. Unless the cycle of impunity is broken and the country's deep-rooted issues are dispassionately confronted, Fiji's quest for reconciliation and justice will likely remain hollow objectives and elusive goals for the foreseeable future.

Works Cited

Asia Pacific Forum of National Human Rights Institutions (APF). 2007. Forum Councilor's Meeting: Twelfth Annual Report. Sydney.

Bloomfield, David. 2006. *On Good Terms: Clarifying Reconciliation.* Berghof Report No. 14. Berlin: Berghof Research Center for Constructive Conflict Management.

Chang, Kevin. 2004. *Noqu Kalou, Noqu Vanua: The Root Causes of Fiji's Societal Conflicts*. Unpublished Master of Arts Thesis. Sydney: Centre for Peace and Conflict Studies, University of Sydney.

—. 2004. "The Challenges of Reconciliation: Lessons from Fiji's Post-Coup Political Dilemma", *PeaceWrites*. Vol. 2, 2004. Sydney: Centre for Peace and Conflict Studies, University of Sydney.

Citizens' Constitutional Forum (CCF). 2005. *CCF Submission to the Sector Standing Committee on Justice, Law and Order regarding the Promotion of Reconciliation, Tolerance and Unity Bill 2005*. Suva.

Daily Post

—. 25 July 2002. *Fatiaki named Chief Justice.*

—. 6 July 2004. *National Day of Prayer and Fasting*. Ministry of National Reconciliation and Unity Advertisement.

Daye, Russell. 2003. "Finding a Model of Reconciliation", *Fijian Studies*, Vol. 1, No. 1, pp 177-192.

Ecumenical Centre for Research, Advocacy and Education (ECREA). 2001. *General Elections: Factors and Outcomes*, Suva (http://www.ecrea.org.fj/webpages/publications_files/Papers/18.doc, accessed December 28, 2006).

Fiji. 2000. *Blueprint for the Protection of Fijian & Rotuman Rights and Interests, and the Advancement of Their Development*. Presentation to the Great Council of Chiefs by Interim Prime Minister Laisenia Qarase, 13 July 2000, Suva.

Fiji. 2002. *50/50 by Year 2020" 20-Year Development Plan (2001-2020) for the Enhancement of Participation of Indigenous Fijians and Rotumans in the Socio-Economic Development of Fiji.* Parliamentary Paper No. 73 of 2002, Suva.

Fiji. 2005. *Healing Fiji Through Restorative Justice: A New Way to Reconciliation and Forgiveness*. Government Advertisement by Laisenia Qarase, Suva.

Fiji. 2007. *PM Bainimarama - Statement at the 38th Pacific Islands Forum Leaders Meeting*. Nuku'alofa, Tonga, October 17, 2007.

Fiji Human Rights Commission (FHRC). 2005. *Submission on Promotion of Reconciliation, Tolerance and Unity Bill 2005 (Bill No 10/2005) to the Parliamentary Sector Standing Committee on Justice, Law and Order*. Suva.

Fiji Human Rights Commission (FHRC). 2006. *Report on Government's Affirmative Action Programmes, 2020 Plan for Indigenous Fijians and Rotumans, and the Blueprint*. Suva.

Fiji Human Rights Commission (FHRC). 2007a. *The Assumption of Executive Authority on December 5th 2006 by Commodore J.V. Bainimarama, Commander of the Republic of Fiji Military Forces: Legal, Constitutional and Human Rights Issues*. Report by Shaista Shameem, Director FHRC. Suva.

Fiji Human Rights Commission (FHRC). 2007b. *A Response to the Fiji Human Rights Commission Director's Report on "The Assumption of Executive Authority by Commodore J.V. Bainimarama, Commander of the Republic of Fiji Military Forces."* Suva.

Fiji Islands Bureau of Statistics. 2006. *2006 Facts at a Glance*. Suva (http://www.statsfiji.gov.fj, accessed January 10, 2007).

Fiji Labour Party (FLP). 2005. *Bill a Contemptuous Challenge to the Judiciary*. FLP Media Release, May 21, 2005, Suva (http://www.flp.org.fj/n050521.htm, accessed January 8, 2007).

Fiji Law Society (FLS). 2005. *Law Society Rejects Unity Bill*. Media Release, June 16, 2005, Suva.

Fijiive (http://fijilive.com) June 13, 2005. *Hindu organization opposes Fiji Reconciliation Bill* (accessed December 13, 2006).

Fiji Police. 2006. *Media Update January 5, 2006: Coup Investigations*. Suva (http://www.police.gov.fj/release5ajan.html, accessed November 28, 2006).

Fiji Times

—. February 15, 2003. *The need to review reconciliation.*

—. August 3, 2004. *"Fijians want Native leader".*

—. January 9,2006. *Fiji Military Commander Warns Government.*

—. August 25, 2006. *Coup probe costs $4m.*

—. January 5, 2007. *Statement by President Josefa Iloilo.*

—. March 22,2007. *Draft Plan of Action, Department Told.*

—. November 22, 2007. *PM's Office Clarifies Charter Development.*

International Center for Transitional Justice (ICTJ). 2006. Reconciliation. (http://www.ictj.org/en/tj/784.html, accessed on May 25, 2007).

International Institute for Democracy and Electoral Assistance (IDEA). 2003. *Reconciliation After Violent Conflict: A Handbook*. Stockholm.

Kurer, Oskar. 2001. "Land and Politics in Fiji: of Failed Land Reforms and Coups," *The Journal of Pacific History*, Vol. 36, No. 3, 2001, pp 299-315.

Lal, Brij V. 1992. *Broken Waves: A History of the Fiji Islands in the Twentieth Century*. Pacific Islands Monograph Series, No. 11. Honolulu: University of Hawai'i Press.

—. 2006. *Islands of Turmoil: Elections and Politics in Fiji*. Canberra: Australian National University E Press.

Madraiwiwi, Joni. 2007. *Mythic Constitutionalism: Whither Fiji's Course in June, 2007?* Paper presented at "The Fiji Coup–Six Months On" Workshop, Australian National University, Canberra, June 5, 2007.

Ministry of National Reconciliation and Unity (MNRU). 2002. *Fiji: A Country in Reconciliation*. MNRU public pamphlet.

Naidu, Vijay. 2006. *The State of the State in Fiji: Some Failings in the Periphery*. In Stewart Firth (ed.), *Globalisation and Governance in the Pacific Islands*. Canberra: Australian National University E Press.

Pacific Magazine. July 12, 2005. *FIJI: Military Says It Will Remove Government, If Bill Is Passed.*

Prasad, Satendra; Dakuvula, Jone and Snell, Darryn. 2001. *Economic Development, Democracy and Ethnic Conflict in the Fiji Islands*, Minority and Development Macro Study, Citizens' Constitutional Forum and Minority Rights Group International.

Qarase, Laisenia. 2000. *National Reconciliation: The Way Forward for Fiji*. Address at the National Tourism Forum, Warwick Hotel, Coral Coast, December 7, 2000.

Radio New Zealand International (RNZI) (http://www.rnzi.com)

—. December 16, 2002. *Fiji Labour Party calls for sacking of senator over racist comments* (accessed December 28, 2006)

—. April 15, 2005. *Fiji Law Society criticizes release of jailed ministers* (accessed January 7, 2007).

Ratuva, Steven. 1998. "Towards Multiculturalism and Affirmative Action: A Case for Fiji", in Jill Cottrell (ed). *Educating for Multiculturalism*. Suva: Citizens' Constitutional Forum.

—. 2002. "God's Will in Paradise: the Politics of Ethnicity and Religion in Fiji," *Development Bulletin*, Vol. 59, October 2002, pp 19-23. Canberra: Development Studies Network, Australian National University.

Reddy, Mahendra and Prasad, Biman. 2002. "Affirmative Action Policies and Poverty Alleviation in Fiji: An Examination of Post-Coup Policies and Programs," *Development Bulletin,* Vol. 60, December 2002. Canberra: Development Studies Network, Australian National University.

Reddy, Mahendra and Naidu, Vijay. 2001. "Land tenure system in Fiji: the poverty implications of expiring leases," *Development Bulletin*, Vol.

55, July 2001. Canberra: Development Studies Network, Australian National University.

Republic of Fiji Military Forces (RFMF). 2007. *Commander RFMF Commodore Voreqe Bainimarama Handover Speech*. RFMF Press Statement, January 4, 2007, Suva.

Rigby, Andrew. 2001. *Justice and Reconciliation: After the Violence*. Boulder/London: Rienner.

Robertson, R and Sutherland, W. 2002. *Government by the Gun: the Unfinished Business of Fiji's 2000 Coup*. Sydney: Pluto Press.

Shameem, Shaista. Personal Communication. November 18, 2007.

Srebrnik, Henry. 2002. "Ethnicity, Religion and the Issue of Aboriginality in a Small Island State: Why Does Fiji Flounder?" *The Round Table*, Vol. 364, pp 187-210.

Sriskandarajah, Dhananjayan. 2003. "Inequality and conflict in Fiji: From purgatory to hell?" *Asia Pacific Viewpoint*, Vol. 44, No. 3, pp 305-324.

Tedeschi, Mark. 2005. "Prosecuting in Paradise—Race, Politics and the Rule of Law in Fiji," *Crime, Law & Social Change*, Vol. 44, pp 79–109.

United Nations Committee on the Elimination of Racial Discrimination (UNCERD). 2003. *Concluding observations of the Committee on the Elimination of Racial Discrimination: Fiji*. 02/06/2003. CERD/C/62/CO/3, Geneva.

United Nations Development Program (UNDP). 1997. *Fiji Poverty Report*. Suva.

Yabaki, Akuila. 2004. *CCF Position on National Reconciliation Process*. Suva: Citizens' Constitutional Forum.

LIST OF CONTRIBUTORS

Barbara Watson Andaya is a professor of Asian Studies and Director of the Center for Southeast Asia Studies at the University of Hawai'i at Manoa. Her current research is on women and gender in early modern Southeast Asia and social issues in contemporary Southeast Asia. She received the Guggenheim Award in 2000 and served as President of the Association for Asian Studies in 2005-2006. Her latest publication is *The Flaming Womb: Repositioning Women in Early Modern Southeast Asia* (Honolulu: University of Hawai'i Press, 2006).

Kevin Chang is a Research Scholar at the Centre for Peace and Conflict Studies, University of Sydney, where he specializes in reconciliation, transitional justice and human rights in post-conflict societies. He has a M.A. in Peace and Conflict Studies from the University of Sydney, writing his thesis on the root causes of Fiji's political conflicts. He followed his M.A. by working as a Research Officer in Fiji's Ministry of National Reconciliation and Unity during 2003-4 under an AusAID assignment. Kevin also has a Graduate Diploma in International Law from the University of Sydney, and a B.Sc. from Monash University. Aside from Fiji, Kevin has previously worked in the Australian Government on indigenous reconciliation policy, and with UNHCR after the Pakistan Earthquake of October 2005. He is currently based in Geneva working for the United Nations Development Program. E-mail: kevin_c_chang@hotmail.com.

Justin Liang is Projects and Outreach Manager at the East-West Center in Washington. He completed his undergraduate degree at Princeton University, earned a Masters from the Australian National University, and was an Asia-Pacific Leadership Fellow at the East-West Center in Honolulu. He has worked as a grassroots volunteer in Micronesia and China and was a researcher at the Crawford School of Economics and Government in Canberra, Australia, and at the National Bureau of Asian Research (NBR) in Washington, DC. He has published on development, policy, and security issues in East Asia and the Pacific.

Rusyan Jill Mamiit-Coburn is a natural resource professional with training and broad experience in conducting economic evaluation and socioeconomic assessment. She has worked extensively with socioeconomic and environmental projects, which involve economic and environmental valuation, cost-benefit analysis, socioeconomic and environmental impact assessment. She is currently pursuing a Ph.D. in Natural Resources and Environmental Management at the University of Hawai'i at Manoa.

Anthea Moore has an honors degree in Economics from the University of New South Wales and a masters degree in international relations from the Australian National University. She has worked for the Australian government as a trade and development economist on free trade agreements, the World Trade Organization and the Group of 20 (G-20) meeting held in Melbourne, Australia in 2006. She also spent a year volunteering as an assistant lecturer in development economics for a masters program in Vietnam. She is currently working on the Australian Government's foreign aid program to Afghanistan. She continues to pursue her interests in the diverse histories and cultures of the Asia Pacific, seeking greater understanding and empowerment of the peoples of the region.

Kiran Sagoo is a Ph.D. candidate in Sociology at the University of Hawai'i at Manoa, USA and has completed a M.A. in Asian Studies, focusing on Southeast Asia. She has received an East-West Center Degree Fellowship and a Fulbright Malaysian Graduate Study and Research Program award. She has a M.Sc. in Comparative Development and International Social Policy from the University of Bristol, United Kingdom and a LLB (Hons) in Law with Economics from the University of Kent at Canterbury, United Kingdom. She has worked as a Program Officer with Consumers International and Health Action International (HAI) based in Malaysia and Sri Lanka. She was the former co-editor of *HAI News*, a newsletter focusing on access to essential medicines and the rational use of medicines. She would like to embark on a career in international development focusing on health development, poverty eradication and conflict resolution.

Wilmar Salim is currently completing his doctoral study in the Department of Urban and Regional Planning, University of Hawai'i at Manoa, USA, under the East-West Center Degree Fellowship. He received a Bachelor of Engineering in Regional and City Planning from Institut Teknologi Bandung, Indonesia and Master of Regional Development from the University of Queensland, Australia. He has authored and co-authored a number of papers for conferences and journals, with a recent publication on "Sustainable livelihood considerations for disaster risk management: Implications for Implementation of the Government of Indonesia Tsunami Recovery Plan", published in *Disaster Prevention and Management, an International Journal* (Spring 2006).

Huong Tran is a community development practitioner, with experience working with grassroots and marginalized people in disadvantaged communities in the South of Vietnam on healthcare, education and community development. She completed a masters program in International Development and Social Change at Clark University, USA in 2007 under the Ford Fellowship. At present, she is working as a freelance consultant on training and community development.

Ha Anh Tuan is currently a research fellow at the Center of Southeast Asian Studies of the Institute of International Relations (IIR) in Hanoi, Vietnam. He also serves as Chairman of this institute's Junior Research Fellows' Club. He gained a masters degree in International Relations at the Australian National University in 2007.

Matt West completed a Master of Philosophy with the Department of Anthropology at the Chinese University of Hong Kong.

Kaushalya Wijayaweera is a sociologist at the IUCN-World Conservation Union in Colombo Sri Lanka. She has been involved in various socioeconomic projects across Sri Lanka.

INDEX